Serious Play

A Leisure Wellness Guidebook

Serious Play

A Leisure Wellness Guidebook

Martin Kimeldorf

TEN SPEED PRESS
Berkeley, California

Ten Speed Press
Box 7123
Berkeley, California 94707

Cover photograph by Jonathan Chester
Cover and text design by Paula Morrison
Typeset by Catherine Campaigne

Library of Congress Cataloging-in-Publication Data

Kimeldorf, Martin.
    Serious play / Martin Kimeldorf.
        p.   cm.
    Includes bibliographical references.
    ISBN 10-89815-630-0
        1. Leisure—Sociological aspects.   2. Play—Sociological aspects.
    3. Sports—Sociological aspects.   4. Leisure—Psychological aspects.
    5. Play—Psychological aspects.   6. Sports—Psychological aspects.
    I. Title.
    GV14.45.K56   1994
    306.4'812—dc20   94-29609
                                                                      CIP

Printed in the United States of America

1   2   3   4   5   —   98   97   96   95   94

ACKNOWLEDGEMENTS

AM INDEBTED TO the following people who encouraged and supported me in the development of this work:

Richard Bolles, author and philosopher about creative, balanced careers

Patsy B. Edwards, author and Owner/Manager of Constructive Leisure

Rozanne W. Faulkner, author and certified therapeutic recreation specialist

Forrest McDowell, author and originator of the idea of "Leisure Wellness"

Curtis Rosler, drug treatment counselor

Doug Spohn, State of Washington Wellness Coordinator

Judy Kimeldorf, my personal leisure guru

The following people played essential roles in editing and revising the first version of this work:

Pam Mortillaro, Sara Yada, and Diane Hills

I feel very fortunate to be working with the Ten Speed gang. I wish to thank George Young for seeing a value in the words I sent him, Mariah Bear for polishing the words until they sparkled, Paula Morrison for her imaginative design, and Leili Eghbal, who enthusiastically helps to spread these words.

Table of Contents

P EOPLE HAVE GREAT interest these days in leading a more balanced life, instead of the workaholic existence we are all too
familiar with. A balanced life includes work, learning, and
leisure.

In learning how to build a more balanced life, the casual reader
can find lots of help in the first two areas. There are a million
books out there about work, and an awful lot about learning.
However, it is not so easy to find help with the leisure component
of a balanced life. There are comparatively few books out about
leisure. This book, therefore, fills a definite need.

My friend Martin Kimeldorf has worked in the arena of leisure
for a long time. He is a gifted teacher and a prolific writer, and
has many useful insights and much guidance to offer, as you will
see.

I do disagree with him in one respect. He says, "A precise definition of leisure has eluded leisure experts for decades." Well, yes
. . . and no. I have been aided for decades by a definition of leisure
that my friend, the late John Crystal, gave to me.

"Leisure," he used to say, "is what you do when no one's telling
you what to do." I broaden "no one" to include "no event," "no
duty," and "no obligation." That definition immediately stakes
out for leisure an important role in this workaholic world in which
we live. To be sure, what we do when no one's telling us what to
do may be simply *to sleep*. Or simply *to goof off,* and move without purpose or aim throughout the day, like some random atom
of steam coming out of a boiling tea kettle. But sometimes what
we choose to do when no one's telling us what to do, when we
are obligated to no person, no duty, no event, is not so random
or aimless as we suppose.

When it is an activity, a pursuit, a hobby, or whatever, that
we pursue in our leisure, I believe we have often chosen this in

obedience to some deep instinct within us, some irresistible urge imbedded in our very nature, that we may give utterance to some God-given talents that are dying to be used but were finding no expression anywhere else in our lives. *Leisure, then, is a mirror where our inner nature stands most revealed.* We are free to do what we were put into this world to do—even though it may be in an embryonic, elementary, or even distorted form.

Career counselors have known this for decades. I recall a woman counselor who was working with a teenage young adult from the ghetto, trying to help him choose a life's work by identifying his skills. He would have none of it.

"I have no skills," he said.

"Well," said his counselor, "what do you do in your leisure time?"

"Nuthin," he persisted.

"Oh come on," she said, "you must do something."

"Nope," he said, "I just watch TV."

"Well, what do you do when you watch TV? I mean, do you stay on one channel, or do you flip channels?"

"I flip channels," he said.

"How do you do that? I mean, do you press a remote, or do you turn knobs?"

"I turn knobs," he said.

"Well, that's using your hands. Do you like using your hands a lot?" she asked.

He thought about it a moment, then said, "Yes, I guess."

She pursued this line of inquiry with him, finding out what else he liked to do with his hands, and ultimately she was able to help him choose a career where he got the chance to use those talents that were in his hands.

But, note well, she began with his leisure activities—as so many wise career counselors do when working with the baffled and perplexed—because she knew that in his leisure his inner nature stood most clearly revealed.

Leisure *wellness*, of which Martin speaks at length, is dependent on this ancient wisdom: that some of our nature's deepest

instincts are revealed in our leisure, developed in our leisure, nur-
tured in our leisure. And it is for this reason that in our leisure
we are most healed, most restored, most vitalized. It is in our
leisure that we are made well.

   To search for such leisure is a rewarding task. And the diligent
reader who pursues the serious work that this book outlines will
indeed find it—I know. I leave you in good hands, Martin's hands.

—Richard N. Bolles
Author, *What Color Is Your Parachute?*

ADMIT IT, I'M a workaholic.

That's why I wrote this book—to remind myself that I work to live, rather than living to work. The tips and exercises in this book have helped me achieve a better balance between my work and my leisure life, and I invite you to discover how they can help anyone who's looking for a healthier approach to using their free time.

As a workaholic, I have spent much of my career consumed with projects. However, upon reaching midlife, several traumatic events forced me to reexamine my lifestyle and my attitudes towards work and play. I now view time as a precious, nonrenewable natural resource. More than ever, I deeply appreciate the fact that each of us is given only a limited amount of time on this planet.

Today, I firmly believe that one's leisure time is really a gift from time's treasure chest. What each of us chooses to do in our free time will either impoverish or enrich our souls. I hope that in reading this book you will unlock or rediscover your own treasures as you rummage through the precious jewels among your past and present experiences, as well as finding entirely new leisure possibilities for the future.

Many of the ideas you will read were first outlined in my book *Pathways to Leisure,* which showed young adults how to apply job-finding techniques to the search for meaningful leisure opportunities.

I later expanded on this theme to create a "Pathways to Leisure Wellness" workshop featuring, among other things, playful games and a bubble-blowing gun. It was a lot of fun, and created a mood that encouraged creative thinking. It quickly became clear that a wider range of people would benefit from—and enjoy—leisure wellness and so, after some research into retirement and aging, *Serious Play* took shape on my computer screen.

Using This Book

Though the topic is leisure, the search for leisure wellness doesn't happen in a leisurely fashion. You must actually work at changing your attitude toward leisure time if you expect to see any change.

In the following chapters, I'll show you how to (re)ignite a passionate interest in the quality of your leisure life. You'll begin by assessing your own level of leisure wellness, and then how you view time in general. Next, we'll take a look at how the notion of work and leisure ethics evolved in this country.

These first steps set the stage for a deeper investigation into your own leisure values, preferences, and interests through an exercise called the *leisure search,* a simple method of applying proven job-hunting techniques to the search for rewarding leisure opportunities in your own community; you'll learn how to find local people and organizations who share your interests.

Separate chapters are devoted to the side issues of time awareness and retirement planning, with exercises created especially to help you analyze your schedule and find new sources of free time. Other exercises will help you develop more flexible attitudes toward the wide range of leisure choices available today.

Try doing the exercises in this book with a group, class, or partner to double the fun and enhance the rewards of your leisure search.

When you take a serious look at how you use your time, both your attitude and the actual experience of time are bound to change. This change may embrace small shifts in your daily routines, or it can mean the kind of large direction-changing decisions that will allow you to live your life in new and more fulfilling ways. In one way or another, the playfulness you once experienced as a child may gradually wend its way back into your adult life.

If these notions sound appealing, *Serious Play* is absolutely the right book for you.

—Martin Kimeldorf
Tumwater, Washington 1994

CHAPTER 1

Getting Serious about Play

ET'S GET SERIOUS: either you play now ... or you pay later! Life is short and not always so sweet, and leisure will be the essential condiment for spicing the brew.

But our leisure time is all too often unfulfilling. Frequently, the way that time is spent (one's "leisure lifestyle") just happens without much thought—or satisfaction. Too few of us even think of examining our leisure-time decisions and behaviors. Perhaps we're afraid of what we'd find.

These days, we know that harmful stress results not only from doing too much, but also from doing too little. When work and leisure time are out of balance, one can ping-pong back and forth between the two extremes, between workaholism and boredom. Put another way, countless people feel that they are either too busy doing something, or too busy doing nothing.

Take a look at your life. Is your leisure time sacrificed to overwork? Is it part of a deadly dull routine, in which every event seems to be played out on a flattened landscape? Perhaps you're one of the few who spend all of their free time and energy on a single mania like jogging, reading, or yardwork. Or, at the other end of the spectrum, does a lack of ideas leave you sitting idly by asking, "What can I do?"

At this point, some readers will say, "Sure, that describes my situation, and I'd love to enjoy my leisure more, but I have no free time, and no money to spend on new activities." But, while a lack of time or money *may* preclude long vacations or certain types of exciting weekends, I *do* want to emphasize that whether or not you have fulfilling leisure time need not depend on how much time or money you have. In fact, the greater fulfillment may come from learning to recreate and renew yourself using resources you already have at your disposal. More is not always better for you—or the planet.

In fact, the quality of your leisure time may best be measured by noticing those unpredictable moments of spare time that spontaneously erupt within even the busiest schedules. They may take the form of an unanticipated work break, downtime between chores, an unexpected delay in traffic, or some quiet time at the beginning or end of a day. Use these pauses in your hectic life to notice your surroundings, people-watch, scribble a short note in a journal, review your weekend plans, or simply try to focus on the emptiness and restfulness of the pause.

Adding new excitement to your leisure time will help you restore sweetness and balance to your life as a whole, but you must be willing to put time and energy into examining, re-creating, and improving your leisure life. You'll need to seriously examine how you play. As George Bernard Shaw put it, people do not cease to play because they grow old, people grow old because they cease to play.

Getting Serious about Work and Play

Many of us are very serious about our careers, to the point of relying on them for our identities. At a party, when a stranger turns to you and asks "So, what do you do?" you probably answer with your job title or place of work. But what we do to live should not necessarily be the same as what we do for a "living." It's time to start responding to this question with what we do for *play* as well as for pay. Greater balance comes from taking our work more lightly and our play more seriously.

People who have this sort of work/leisure balance often reap unexpected career or business rewards, as many opportunities can spring from mutual leisure interests. For example, imagine that, while in a job interview, you notice a picture of a bike race on the employer's wall. You mention that you have done some cross-country cycling, and the bond is established. When it comes time to make the final hiring decision, a warm remembrance of your common interest in bicycles can put you in front of the pack.

Businesspeople often form important contacts through service-club work, or while discussing hobbies and leisure interests at social gatherings. Large corporations give box-seat tickets for sporting or cultural events to favored clients ... *not* tickets to seminars on Total Quality Management.

More and more employers are recognizing the value of integrating playfulness and humor into the workplace. Consultants teach managers and line-staff how to insert humor into the corporate culture, using it as a vent for stressful situations as well as to enhance creativity.

Levity has even been shown to measurably increase productivity. Employees who use humor to free themselves from conventional thinking and solutions tend to take a more creative approach to problem-solving and team-building. Flexible attitudes are built upon playfulness.

Imagine a group of people trying to draft the mission statement for an important project. You've almost certainly seen such tasks bogged down in endless bickering, tedium, and nonproductive discussions. Suppose instead everyone paired up and discussed their favorite comedy and comedian. Then each pair could take turns sharing how their favorite comedian might go about drafting the mission statement. Once laughter is injected, people become more accepting of one another's contributions. This works in a variety of situations, as brainstorming sessions always work better when the participants are given permission—and encouragement—to think unconventionally at first.

Laughing Your Way to Wellness

Health practitioners have also noticed the beneficial effects of an injection of humor. Studies show that laughter stimulates production of endorphins, the body's natural painkillers. Jocularity appears to have a healing or calming influence on the cardiovascular, respiratory, and immune systems. In addition, tight muscles relax, pain diminishes, and digestion improves.

All of this underscores comedian Josh Billings's observation that, "There ain't much fun in medicine, but there's a heck of a lot of medicine in fun." These days, more and more hospitals agree, and are trying to bring humor and playfulness into the practice of medicine. Some organizations have created "humor carts" filled with silly sight gags, toys, and humorous reading material. These carts are pushed from bed to bed in an effort to lift the patients' spirits with healing laughter, instead of drugs.

Laughing at Yourself—for Survival

Laughing at ourselves and our experiences may help us through those difficult situations that we often cannot change. Walk into any school or hospital lounge and you'll hear the staff laughing as they tell the day's stories. Humor creates breathing room in any environment saturated with stress.

Most comedy revolves around human imperfections. If you repress or deny the value of humor and playfulness at work, you will be left with unrealistic expectations of perfect performance, expectations that can generate stress, fear, and anxiety.

Humor, or a playful attitude, can mean a break from routine. When we laugh at our jobs, procedures, personal habits, customs, or rituals, we free ourselves from the prison of daily conformity, as well as from our inhibitions. People who can laugh at their own foibles are more accepting of themselves, and less likely to become envious or overly judgmental. Humor gives us a perspective on the conditions and relationships which dominate our lives at work, at home, or in the community at large.

Becoming a Professional Amateur

There is another side to this humor-and-play equation. While many people feel that the amount of time they have for leisure activities has decreased, Kimeldorf's Hypothesis #1 suggests that, instead, "as we age, we often mourn the loss of our playful attitude, and mistakenly call it a loss of leisure time."

Along these lines, you may discover that a quality of playfulness in your life seems to disappear because our work ethics or attitudes often slew over into what should be recreation time. Witold Rybczynski outlines this problem in his book *Waiting for the Weekend,* in which he looks at the language we use to describe our play. People often talk about "working out" or "working at one's game," rather than using phrases which emphasize enjoyment or experimentation.

Do you wear "professional quality" outfits on the tennis court, to the beach, or while backpacking? By dressing for success in the leisure world, you may have cloaked your sense of play.

There are many ways to change this. One alternative is to honor your "amateur" status. The word *amateur* is built from the root word meaning "lover." Most amateur sportspeople, for example, consider playing and connecting with others more important than competing to win. The next time you play tennis, go dancing, or shoot pictures, try thinking of yourself as an amateur. Enjoy the sloppiness and rough edges. Get out onto the tennis court in cut-off jeans, take your pictures with a very cheap camera, go hiking with an old wicker basket instead of a high-tech backpack.

Substance Abuse Follows from Time Abuse

Kimeldorf's Hypothesis #2 states, "a substance abuse illness often goes hand-in-hand with a diseased leisure." In fact, most people who abuse drugs do so during their leisure time.

People who abuse drugs are people who, consciously or unconsciously, place a low value on leisure activities and free time. Their leisure becomes one-dimensional, and is reserved as a time for abuse or escape. After becoming addicted, the individual can't comprehend enjoying leisure time without drugs. The user chooses friends and partners with similar interests (or lack of interests). The addiction drains meaning and vitality from free-time experiences, leaving behind an emptiness that must be constantly filled with drugs. Rehabilitation programs that help their clients revitalize their leisure lifestyles provide an invaluable alternative to the lure of drugs. Counselor Curt Rosler demonstrates how he integrated leisure wellness into his drug treatment program in Appendix C, "Using Leisure Wellness in Drug Treatment."

Playful Seniors

We all recognize humor and play as crucial ingredients of a happy childhood. Elwood Chapman, an authority on retirement and living well in later years, points out that playfulness is also extremely important in our later years. Many gifted older citizens have demonstrated that eccentric behavior is the antidote to a premature rocking-chair existence. Chapman and others exhort senior citizens to express their individuality through such simple things as their choice of clothing or their comportment and posture. One poet talks about abandoning the sobriety of her youth by wearing more purple in old age, a dance instructor encourages her eighty-year-olds to put a spring in their strides, and a therapist encourages people to dress up their wheelchairs and wear sandals! Cheer the sounds of shattered stereotypes!

One exemplary senior quoted in Chapman's book reflects, "If I had my life to live over, I'd dare to make more mistakes ... I would be sillier than I have been this trip." She cautions against living life too seriously. Yet, at the same time she encourages us to seriously pursue the qualities of playfulness. She concludes that people who are more playful probably can cope with real problems, and experience far fewer imaginary troubles.

What Is This Thing Called Leisure?

With this discussion of playfulness as a background curtain, it is time to step forward and begin your study of leisure. The perspective of an amateur and the gift of laughter should help you feel free enough to take an honest look at your leisure preferences, interests, and attitudes—without worrying what others find "acceptable."

Look in a mirror, study that funny and wondrous face. Consider the stories you wear behind your mask. Grant yourself permission to play. Then begin the task of defining what leisure means to you. This begins the first step in practicing serious play.

One of this book's most important goals is that of helping you develop your own highly personalized definition of leisure. You will begin by examining the word. Later, you'll read the author's definition. By the end of this book, you'll have created a personal definition to use as a guide in setting your new leisure course. Begin now by completing Exercise One.

Exercise 1:
Defining Leisure

Write your definition of what leisure is and isn't in the space provided below. Each part of your definition must contain two examples from your life.

1. Describe what leisure is or includes.

_____

_____

_____

Two examples in my life would be:

_____

_____

2. Describe what leisure is not.

_____

_____

_____

Two examples in my life would be:

_____

_____

If you were to compare your definition to several other people's, you might be surprised at the unique way each person has of looking at leisure.

This shouldn't come as too much of a shock, however. After all, a precise definition of leisure has eluded experts in the field for decades. For example, think about the act of letter writing. Some people see writing any letter as work, or a chore, while others see it as an enjoyable leisure-time activity. Clearly, the definition of "leisure" cannot rely on examining individual activities by themselves. Instead, you must examine the context in which each takes place (writing letters at work versus at home) as well as your attitude towards the specific activity.

A Quiz-i-cal Look at Leisure

It is easy to take the concept of leisure for granted. For instance, do you feel that most people spend a great deal of time watching television or reading a newspaper? The following quiz will help you examine your assumption.

Exercise 2:
How Do People Spend Their Leisure Time?

Circle what you believe are the correct answers to these true-or-false questions. Then we'll review your answers and learn what researchers found when they surveyed people in different countries.

1. T F People in different parts of the country spend their leisure time differently.

2. T F People in the U.S. spend more time watching television than citizens of any other nation.

3.   T   F   As people put in shorter workweeks, they tend to spend more hours in leisure.

4.   T   F   People in the U.S. spend more time reading books than people in any other nation.

5.   T   F   People who spend more hours in leisure claim to have greater job satisfaction.

Affluence versus Fulfillment

If the truth be known, there are some broad similarities in how Americans spend their leisure time. But, many of our assumptions about leisure begin to break down when we compare our use of free time to that of people in different countries. This is complicated by the fact that work, leisure, and success may be viewed differently in different cultures.

For instance, while people in the United States often wish to emulate Japan's economic prowess, the use of leisure time in Japan forces us to reexamine the ultimate definition of the word "success." Reports of a country's rising gross national product (GNP), productivity, and profitability may reveal nothing about its quality of life once the charts are taken down, the board rooms closed, and people head home.

While no one can dispute Japan's achievements in the work world, these achievements do not appear to make life much easier or more leisurely for its citizens. This irony is most pronounced in the case of leisure choices open to women.

Statistics from a study conducted by Peter Seidman at the University of Michigan make some interesting comparisons. These results were reported in a press release on April 6, 1990. The data summarized in the following chart shows that Japanese men spend more time at work than the average male in the U.S.

At the same time, Japanese women spend the most hours per week doing housework and watching TV. And together, Japanese men and women watch more TV than the people in any other country in this study. While watching TV in and of itself is not

an unhealthy leisure choice, it is hardly a sign of superior achievement in terms of a balanced approach to work and play.

These findings in the chart bring up two essential questions:
Is there a limit to the benefits of increasing work productivity and
GNP? And, when comparing the quality of life in different coun-
tries, what factors besides economics should be considered?

Activity Hours Spent:	Gender	U.S.	Japan
In leisure and play	men	20.5	13.3
	women	21.8	10.6
At work and commuting	men	44	52
	women	25.9	25.8
Doing housework	men	13.8	3.5
	women	26	31
Watching TV	men	12.3	17
	women	11.5	21.4

Answers to Quiz

The data above may jar some of your leisure stereotypes. Likewise, comparing your responses in Exercise Two to the correct
answers may help you reexamine some of your assumptions.

1. F Most studies show that people generally spend their
free time similarly.

2. F The Japanese watch more TV than people of any other
nation.

3. F Surprisingly, not everyone uses the extra time for leisure.
As the workweek begins to shorten, several studies show
that people use the extra time to get a second job.

4. F Compared to other nations Americans may spend more
time reading newspapers, but not books.

5. T People who report spending more of their nonwork
hours involved in their leisure also report greater rates
of satisfaction with their job. Moreover, they report
greater satisfaction with life in general.

Exercise 3:
The Leisure Wellness Survey

Like a thermometer, the following survey gauges your relative leisure health and wellness. To help renew your playfulness, however, it uses a quiz or game format to do so. In concert with the spirit of frivolity, no claim is made for the scientific validity of this survey. However, most people who have taken this quiz during my workshops report that their findings, or ratings, appear to be accurate or personally meaningful.

The Kimeldorf Leisure Wellness Survey

This is not a test, but rather a survey of your opinions, which will help you assess your leisure attitudes and values in five different areas or clusters: your physical condition, use of free time, interactions with others, how you make decisions, and the value of your free time.

Directions

Read each statement below. If you think the statement is true most of the time for you, then put a ☒ in the Yes box. If it is usually not true put the ☒ in the No box. Read each statement carefully. Note that the Yes and No boxes switch back and forth from Column A to Column B. Please answer honestly. There are no right or wrong answers.

#1: My Physical Condition

Column A   Column B

1. Yes ☐ No ☐ I exercise three or more times a week.
2. Yes ☐ No ☐ I think my weight is normal for my age and height.
3. No ☐ Yes ☐ I often oversleep, or stay in bed a long time after waking up.
4. Yes ☐ No ☐ Most years, I have fewer than three serious colds.

5. No ☐ Yes ☐   I often find it difficult to get to sleep.

6. No ☐ Yes ☐   I often don't get enough sleep.

7. No ☐ Yes ☐   When I eat, I usually overeat.

#2: *Using My Free Time*

8. No ☐ Yes ☐   I often fill my "free time" with chores or busy work.

9. No ☐ Yes ☐   I generally do my leisure activities at scheduled intervals.

10. No ☐ Yes ☐   When I have nothing to do, I often feel nervous or uneasy.

11. No ☐ Yes ☐   On most days, I watch TV for two or more hours.

12. No ☐ Yes ☐   Smoking, drinking, or doing drugs helps me to relax.

#3: *Me and Others in Free Time*

13. No ☐ Yes ☐   I often like to spend time alone or away from others.

14. Yes ☐ No ☐   I enjoy spending some of my leisure hours around others.

15. No ☐ Yes ☐   I often feel lonely in my free time.

16. No ☐ Yes ☐   I often avoid people in my free time.

17. No ☐ Yes ☐   For some reason, the most important people in my life don't understand or know about my leisure desires or interests.

#4: *Deciding What to Do*

18. No ☐ Yes ☐   Other people usually dictate what I do in my spare time.

19. Yes ☐ No ☐   I keep up on local or community events I can participate in.

20. No ☐ Yes ☐ Most of my leisure interests cost more than I can afford.

21. Yes ☐ No ☐ I feel that I plan my leisure time well.

22. Yes ☐ No ☐ I enjoy learning new things in my spare time.

23. No ☐ Yes ☐ I need more ideas on how to spend my free time.

24. No ☐ Yes ☐ I know what I want to do, but I often don't know how to get started, or where to find out about it.

#5: The Value of My Free Time

25. Yes ☐ No ☐ What I do in leisure is as important as what I do at work.

26. No ☐ Yes ☐ Like other parts of my life, my leisure is often boring.

27. No ☐ Yes ☐ I often cannot enjoy my leisure time when I am experiencing stress or unhappiness in other parts of my life (work, family, relationships, etc.).

28. Yes ☐ No ☐ I have found that my leisure time helps me to grow or feel more satisfied with my life.

Scoring and Analyzing the Wellness Survey

The following two-step analysis process will make this survey even more useful for you.

Step 1: Deriving a Total Score

The marks in Column A tend to indicate areas of leisure wellness for most people. These are the areas you definitely want to maintain. The marks in Column B indicate areas in which you may wish to consider making changes.

Total score (number of marks in the A Column): _____

Rating:

15 or less	Low level of leisure wellness
16–22	Average leisure wellness
23 or higher	High level of leisure wellness and satisfaction

If, based on your experience and personal values, you feel your score is inaccurate, examine your answers to see if a given question might not apply to your unique situation. For instance, question number 13 states, "I often like to spend time alone or away from others." Generally, this is given a negative score because it indicates a desire for isolation. However, if you spend a lot of time with people while at work you might prefer to spend most of your leisure time alone. Then revise your score by adding a point for that question (as though it was marked in the A column). Determine if this revision more accurately reflects your leisure wellness.

Step 2: Analyze the General Areas to Change and Maintain.
Analyze your survey responses from the different wellness areas. Looking at how you responded in a given area of the test can help you to more specifically identify your leisure wellness strengths and areas of concern. Go back and look at your scores in each of the five cluster areas. Try to determine which areas appear to be your strongest and weakest.

My strongest leisure wellness area to maintain would probably be:
(Hint: where are most of the "A" column marks?)

☐ My Physical Condition

☐ Using My Free Time

☐ Me and Others in Free Time

☐ Deciding What to Do

☐ The Value of My Free Time

The area I probably need improvement in to achieve greater leisure wellness could be:

(Hint: where are most of the "B" column marks ?)

☐ My Physical Condition

☐ Using My Free Time

☐ Me and Others in Free Time

☐ Deciding What to Do

☐ The Value of My Free Time

Final Words about Your Score

Regardless of the final score, the real purpose of this test is to spark some analysis and thinking about your use of leisure time. You are the ultimate judge of the usefulness, meaning, and fairness of your score. Modify your conclusion based on your own perceptions.

A few weeks after finishing this book, go back and see which items you would change. Changing your score is probably a good indicator that you have thought seriously about your leisure time habits, behavior, and/or attitudes.

In the next two chapters you'll read about the way leisure has changed throughout history. Then, armed with a knowledge of history and your leisure wellness score, you'll be ready to probe deeper into your leisure values, preferences, and options.

CHAPTER 2

The Puzzle of Time

T FIRST, THE notion of leisure may seem to be pretty un-complicated. However, as I pointed out in the first chapter, the very word itself is not so easily defined. Leisure is not simply the opposite of work, because one person's leisure may be another person's chore or job. If you pursue the topic further, you invariably end up contemplating the idea of time itself. The study of leisure can take one down a winding philosophical path that is often both puzzling and paradoxical.

We will examine several connected aspects of leisure time, including:

- Societies in which an increase in material wealth seems to coincide with a decrease in leisure time.
- The various ways we ignore or abuse our leisure moments.
- The contemporary feeling that our lives and particularly our *time* can best be described with words like compression, compartmentalization, and fractionalization.
- How to get more free time.

The Paradox of Increasing Affluence and Decreasing Leisure Time

Many studies show that Americans feel they have less and less free time even though they live in one of the most affluent, high-speed, high-tech societies ever. Why haven't our time-saving gadgets (including faxes, microwaves, computers, cellular phones, and phone answering machines) and labor-saving devices (like power lawn mowers, cars, home gyms) resulted in a giant increase in leisure time?

In large part, the answer lies in the fact that all of these time- and labor-saving gadgets are actually riddled with time traps. While modern appliances like the vacuum and washing machine allow us to clean more quickly, many of us just use the extra time to clean more often and more thoroughly. A hundred years ago, clothes-washing and house-cleaning were done far less frequently, maybe once every few weeks. Most people today do a larger volume of laundry than their parents ever did. We wear clothes for shorter periods between cleaning. The average starter house in the 1990s is twice the size it was in the 1950s. This means twice the cleaning and maintenance.

Most "smart" gadgets today require study before one can master using them. Microwave ovens come with elaborate manuals and special recipes. The constantly upgraded personal digital assistants and electronic datebooks require knowledge of various database procedures before you can use them effectively. As computers get "smarter," they come with an ever expanding library of books, manuals, videotapes, and support services. How many people regularly tape television shows, yet leave their VCR clock displays at "high noon" because they couldn't figure out how to reset it after a power outage? All these toys and tools demand time to study and master. As a result, part of our free time is spent on the learning curve.

If we look beneath the surface of these techno-marvels and examine how we really spend our time, surprising things are revealed. For example, dual wage earning couples and single parents spend more time at work than at home during the week, as they rack up forty- to fifty-five-hour workweeks. Weekends are then used to catch up on chores not yet completed, which means that they tend to be filled with a sense of urgency or drudgery. When, on Monday, coworkers ask, "How was your weekend?" it's hard to brag about doing chores. The weekend is no longer a time to unwind, to relax, to do nothing at all.

Other people feel obligated to spend their weekends doing something special or different. Some double-income families use their spare money to pay for house-cleaning, cooking, elder care, or child-care services. Then they use the spare time they've thus purchased to pursue special events which can be proudly reported on Monday.

The paradox of decreasing free time in the midst of proliferating labor-saving technology is best reflected in the face of the 400 million timepieces mass-produced each year. As French philosopher Michel Serres wryly observes, "Everyone has a watch and no one has the time."

Information Explosion Leads to Collapse of Quality and Time

In the 1970s, we marveled at being able to choose between 175 movies to see, or 11,000 different products in a supermarket. In the 1990s there is talk of choosing from 500 channels of entertainment and 40,000 products brought right into our homes on the information superhighway.

When the Wright brothers originally struggled to get their collection of canvas, rod, and wire up into the air, could they have envisioned the day when the documentation for a Boeing 747 airplane weighs more than the plane itself? The quality of our lives is shaped in large part by an ever-expanding number of choices and an endless flow of information.

In this data-saturated world, the news media try to prevent us from changing channels by offer news-bites every 3.5 seconds. Finally, to gain your attention in this flash flood of information, they rely more and more heavily on sensationalism. Life appears both speeded up and degraded in the process.

Because we're always at high tide, we can no longer keep track of the info-flow. We often can't recall where we got a piece of information, where it's stored, or why we once found it meaningful.

In trying to keep up, we are turning the admirable concept of

lifelong learning into the intellectual component of the information rat-race.

We are bombarded, surrounded, and soaked to our eyeballs
in information, with little chance to digest, integrate, or reflect.
We have little opportunity to process all that we take in, and
thereby lose the opportunity to turn information into knowledge.
As our personal landscapes become bloated with information, we
lose any sense of where we are or who we want to become.

The Bottom Line on Leisure Time

At this point you might ask, "What has happened to our free
time? How much do we actually have today?" Because leisure is
so difficult to define, the research findings remain ambiguous.
Studies at the University of Maryland and the University of Michigan suggest that Americans have about thirty-nine hours of leisure
time each week. On the other hand, a similar survey by the
National Research Center for the Arts reported only about half
as much time, approximately seventeen hours per week.

Another study found that between 1965 and 1981, our total
leisure time increased by about 14 percent. However, upon closer
examination, most studies reveal that the distribution of leisure
opportunities in any society is about as unequal as the distribution of wealth and power. Without laboring the obvious, more
leisure is accrued by affluent families. Not surprisingly, single parents have actually seen a decline in their leisure time.

Sociologist John Robinson has been surveying how Americans
spend their free time for thirty years. From the University of Maryland, he reports that between 1965 and 1975, we gained five hours
of free time per week. He also found a similar increase in the
amount of time spent watching television.

What does all this mean? You'll have to draw your own con-
clusions about the bottom line for leisure, based on common sense
and your particular situation. How you use your leisure time may
be more important than the absolute number of hours you have
at your discretion.

The Problem of Free Time Abuse

Unlike the medieval or ancient cultures in which people lived a very routine existence, our contemporary society offers us a seemingly endless menu of choices for our free time. One day you're vacationing at a resort, the next morning you take in a museum, stop in a coffeehouse for lunch, shop at the mall in the afternoon, and then face a whole new set of choices for dinner and the rest of the evening.

For some people, this cornucopia of options leads to a paralysis. Stung by the question, "Where to begin?" they respond by doing nothing.

This is especially vexing for workaholics, who find it extremely uncomfortable to sit around and do nothing. Thus, when the workaholic is unable to develop a leisure-time agenda, free time is often filled with chores or take-home work. One such individual commented, "I find that I'm still driven, even in my free time. And if I don't give myself something do, like chop wood or clean the gutters, I'll start obsessing about work."

Similarly, people addicted to drugs (instead of work) find the meaningful use of leisure to be equally challenging. One of the first steps in recovery involves an analysis of how one spends free time. Often the patient concludes that much of his or her free time is spent thinking about a drink, a pill, a smoke. In this instance it is easy to see how the abuse of free time leads to chemical abuse.

Whatever the situation, most of us have difficulty gaining an awareness of the negative consequences of wasting or abusing our free time.

Time Becomes Compressed and Fractionalized

Examining the kind of chores we do offers another clue about how the experience of time has changed. In the past, our great-grandparents hauled wood and water, slow and laborious activities. Today, we haul children to Little League or haul groceries onto a bus.

Before you had the convenience of a microwave oven, you

paused to wait for food to defrost. Similarly, at the end of a type-written line you might pause to hit the return lever or insert a new piece of paper. Our chores *and* our free time pursuits were not only simpler, they were less hectic and slower and often included what one author calls "built-in pauses."

Today everything is speeded up. "Smart" appliances not only make things happen automatically; they set the pace for us. Your phone rings, your pager beeps, and you answer like a servant. As a result, we have lost the short opportunities to pause and reflect, to catch our breath. Instead of reading and reflecting as we turn the page, we scroll a screen and scan megabytes of information in the endless flow of electronic mail. People no longer wait and mull things over before the mail arrives. Today, your reply must be instantly faxed or e-mailed. One expert speaks of the "vanishing pause" and the resulting sense of time speeding up.

We have exacerbated this sped-up pace by increasingly trying to do two or more things at once—eating and watching TV, visiting while movies play on the VCR, driving and talking on the phone, taking the laptop computer on vacation, using the speaker phone while cooking. In computer-speak this is called "multi-tasking." But when humans try to multi-task, we never become fully engaged in any of the activities; we feel sped up, and a sense of weariness or exhaustion overtakes us. Still, we keep trying to check things off, until one day we end up in the coronary ward, with an unfinished "to-do" list.

Time-management consultant Jeffrey J. Mayer observes, "We often try to cram in so many activities that we don't give ourselves enough time to enjoy any of them." Americans are obsessed with being productive, and when this carries over into our leisure time we trade stress for renewal.

One look at your congested calendar reveals how your living has been squeezed into these tiny rows of weekly squares. Author Ralph Keyes compares our busy schedules to traffic gridlock, in his book *Timelock*. He observes how our moments are all locked up on our calendars. You may come to view your calendar as a giant filing system for compressed moments.

The sense of compression is not limited to a given calendar month. In the past, one's autobiography contained only a few chapter titles, because many people had a single career, stayed married to the same person, and lived in the same community most of their life. Today, people live through many more episodes, changing jobs, partners, location, families, and houses the way they change their seasonal wardrobes. This quickened pace leaves many people breathless and feeling exhausted. Leisure becomes exclusively an escape into "doing nothing," rather than a time of recreation and refreshment.

The busy person makes highly detailed schedules, cutting up his or her time into smaller and smaller pieces. They inevitably begin to feel fragmented or fractionalized, as though they were living a life of continuous interruptions.

Everything that enhances or facilitates communications further fractionalizes our time. The onslaught of telecommuting, cellular phones, beepers, and call-forwarding means you can be reached anywhere at any time. The experience of a private moment has disappeared beneath the satellite beam that tracks you down and connects you to someone halfway across the continent.

One study showed that the average manager has less than eight minutes of uninterrupted time each day. Soon, the real status symbol will be *not* having a telecommunications device.

Looking for Extra Time

Whether you feel you have less or more free time, or a faster or slower life, almost everyone is looking for extra time. Before you can develop a strategy for creating more free time, you must first figure out exactly how you spend the time that you *do* have now. Just as in any time-management exercise, leisure management begins with a time log.

Most people underestimate the amount of free time at their disposal, and people who take the time to do exercises like the one below are usually surprised by what they find. For instance, John Robinson, a sociologist at the University of Maryland, asked five thousand people to estimate how much free time they had. They typically estimated about twenty hours a week. However, an hour-by-hour review of their time use revealed that most had about twice that amount of free time. This discrepancy resulted from the fact that most respondents tended not to count watching television as free time.

Use the time log in Exercise Four to record everything you do in a few typical days. This is like analyzing a portfolio of investments—only in this instance, you're analyzing your most important nonrenewable asset: time. Once you've done this, you'll be able to analyze your hours the same way you'd analyze a budget. In fact, you'll ask similar questions, like, "How can I save? What can I shift around?" Then, you'll develop a time budget to prioritize, reallocate, or restructure how you spend your time.

Exercise 4:
Time Log Recording Sheet

Use the Time Log below to discover how you use your time. Begin by choosing two days to study, your favorite and least favorite days of the week. Record what you are doing every three to four hours. A sample time log is shown. Make two copies of the log for your best and worst day. You can then analyze it in the following exercises.

Time of Day	What I Did	Who Was Around	Amount
	Two to three times each day pause and record what you have done up to that point. You can use codes by checking off S-sleep, W-Work, and C-Chores. Write in activities which are neither Sleep, Work, or Chores.	Check off A-alone or W-with others. Write in names if you're with someone you like.	Write in estimated cost, if any.
	S W C	A W	$
1 A.M.	☐ ☐ ☐ _____	☐ ☐ _____	_____
2	☐ ☐ ☐ _____	☐ ☐ _____	_____
3	☐ ☐ ☐ _____	☐ ☐ _____	_____
4	☐ ☐ ☐ _____	☐ ☐ _____	_____
5	☐ ☐ ☐ _____	☐ ☐ _____	_____
6	☐ ☐ ☐ _____	☐ ☐ _____	_____
7	☐ ☐ ☐ _____	☐ ☐ _____	_____
8	☐ ☐ ☐ _____	☐ ☐ _____	_____
9	☐ ☐ ☐ _____	☐ ☐ _____	_____
10	☐ ☐ ☐ _____	☐ ☐ _____	_____
11	☐ ☐ ☐ _____	☐ ☐ _____	_____
12 noon	☐ ☐ ☐ _____	☐ ☐ _____	_____
1 P.M.	☐ ☐ ☐ _____	☐ ☐ _____	_____
2	☐ ☐ ☐ _____	☐ ☐ _____	_____
3	☐ ☐ ☐ _____	☐ ☐ _____	_____
4	☐ ☐ ☐ _____	☐ ☐ _____	_____
5	☐ ☐ ☐ _____	☐ ☐ _____	_____
6	☐ ☐ ☐ _____	☐ ☐ _____	_____
7	☐ ☐ ☐ _____	☐ ☐ _____	_____
8	☐ ☐ ☐ _____	☐ ☐ _____	_____
9	☐ ☐ ☐ _____	☐ ☐ _____	_____
10	☐ ☐ ☐ _____	☐ ☐ _____	_____
11	☐ ☐ ☐ _____	☐ ☐ _____	_____
12 A.M.	☐ ☐ ☐ _____	☐ ☐ _____	_____

Sample

	S W C		A W		$
...					
5	☒ ☐ ☐ _____		☐ ☐ _____		_____
6	☐ ☐ ☒ _Dress, shower, put out dog_		☐ ☒ _Fido_		_____
7	☐ ☐ ☒ _Commute_		☐ ☒ _Helen_		$1.50
8	☐ ☒ ☐ _____		☐ ☐ _____		_____
9	☐ ☒ ☐ _____		☐ ☐ _____		_____
10	☐ ☐ ☐ _Take break—15 minutes_		☐ ☐ _____		_____
11	☐ ☒ ☐ _____		☐ ☐ _____		_____
12 noon	☐ ☐ ☐ _Lunch—sack_		☐ ☒ _Steve_		$1.00
1 P.M.	☐ ☒ ☐ _Attend seminar training till 4_		☐ ☐ _____		_____
...					
4	☐ ☐ ☒ _Got home early—did chores_		☐ ☐ _____		_____
5	☐ ☐ ☒ _Dinner_		☐ ☐ _____		?
6	☐ ☐ ☒ _Shop for food_		☐ ☐ _____		_____
7	☐ ☐ ☐ _____		☐ ☐ _____		_____
8	☐ ☐ ☐ _Watched soaps I taped_		☐ ☐ _____		_____
9	☐ ☐ ☐ _____		☐ ☐ _____		_____
10	☒ ☐ ☐ _Bed_		☐ ☐ _____		_____

Time Log Analysis

At this point, your time log is filled with data—but what does it mean? How can you use this information to your advantage? First, you can look for patterns that indicate typical time use and abuse. Once you understand these patterns, you can see how to better manage your time in order to create more leisure moments.

The next exercise will help you determine how to squeeze more hours from the face of your clock. Use the following questions to diagnose where you can cut back on wasted efforts, or on activities that are often done out of habit. This process of redesigning how you use your time will free up extra minutes—and perhaps hours.

Exercise 5:
Squeezing Time from the Face of a Clock

During military combat soldiers take leave with R & R or Rest and Relaxation. Today we're in combat with a sped-up culture, and R & R refers to the process of Review and Reflection. The exercises listed next may help you regain a sense of rest and relaxation through a process of review and reflection.

The exercises will help you unwind from the merry-go-round and provide you with a brief respite. They include tips for reorganizing how you use time, and methods for renewing your relationship to time itself. Use or adapt these exercises to creatively squeeze more moments from the face of the clock. Let these magical discoveries fill your treasure chest with the one commodity money can't buy—time.

1. Time problems and desires

List two things you wish you had more time to learn, practice, or enjoy.

a. _____   b. _____

Are you willing to think creatively to squeeze more time from the face of the clock?

☐ yes ... then go on   ☐ no ... forget this page, I need a free moment now!

2. Do you abuse your free moments?

When you get home early and have an extra thirty minutes what do you do? Be honest!

☐ chores   ☐ sleep   ☐ watch TV   ☐ other _____

3. Inventorying your time use

Leisure counselors often advise clients to keep an inventory of their time-use in a time log or diary. One records the daily activities and the relevant information about people, places, costs, and benefits in the time log. Whether you have time to complete a time log, or not, it is helpful to take stock of how you use time. Begin by responding to the four questions that follow. Then, use this information with strategies in Step 4 to begin creating more leisure time.

A. List the four chores you do most frequently. Then list four frequent, routine trips you make around town in an average week.

Chores: Trips:

a. _____   a. _____

b. _____   b. _____

c. _____   c. _____

d. _____   d. _____

B. List three leisure activities you do out of habit or routine, without much thinking (things like always watching a certain television show on a certain night, reading magazines that no longer interest you, or other somewhat aimless experiences).

a. _____

b. _____

c. _____

C. List two things you think are so important that you schedule them or take classes to make sure that you do them (like exercising, being with a partner or family, volunteer work, etc.).

a. _____

b. _____

D. List a project or two you have always wanted to do but just couldn't find the time (like building a deck, writing a book, etc.).

a. _____

b. _____

4. Time-enhancing strategies

These exercises use information from Step 3 to help you find or create new leisure moments.

A. *Changing frequency of chores and trips*

• Review your information about chores and trips under the previous inventory question (3, A). List below any chore you would be willing to do less frequently. List any trips or chores which could be combined to save time. Then estimate the time savings.

Chores: _____ time saved: _____

  _____ _____

  _____ _____

Trips: _____ time saved: _____

  _____ _____

  _____ _____

• How could you rearrange your chore schedule to create little moments throughout the week (stop doing laundry daily and do it once a week) or create a block of time by doing all your little chores (like food shopping) on a single day?

• Recognize that your time is worth money. Be prepared to part with a little bit of your income as a way of retrieving free time. There are people for hire who will clean your house, pick up groceries, create gift baskets, garden, walk your dog, and pay your monthly bills. Suppose you pay a housekeeper to come every other week, and learn to tolerate the mess in between. Some readers will worry about blowing their entertainment budget on a house-cleaner.

Consider the alternatives. You could spend a hectic Saturday cleaning and then racing off to spend the $20 on a newly released movie and the expensive soda and popcorn. Or, you could spend your movie budget to get a housekeeper every other week. While this person cleans, you could visit a park, stroll downtown, and on the way home rent a cheap video. Which choice gets you what you want the most?

List one budget expenditure you could shift to a service provider (gardening, meal preparation, cleaning, etc.):

_____

List what you'd have to give up in order to pay for this:

_____

• Could you trade some chores with other people? Suppose you wanted to take a new painting class, but it is offered at the time when you must pick up your child from day care. Because your neighbor also has a child in that day care center, perhaps you could mow their grass every week in exchange for their picking up your child.

B. Changing leisure habits and daily routines

Look over your answers to Step 3, part B, above. Identify the one activity you do with the least amount of thought. Ask yourself, "Is this leisure activity something I do out of habit or because it is truly fulfilling?" Then use the following questions as motivators for changing your habits and routines.

• Which leisure habit or routine would you be willing to not do next week?

_____

• What could you do instead?

_____

• Can you change any of your daily routines (eating, sleeping, chores) to get more "play time"? Can you get up an hour earlier in order to create an extra hour for a hobby (skip the TV show and go to bed earlier)?

_____

_____

_____

C. Scheduling leisure
List an important leisure activity you often neglect because of your busy schedule.

_____

Now, write it down on your calendar or to-do list so it gets scheduled into your life.

D. Projects
Review the project you identified in Step 3, part D, with the following two questions in mind:

• Can the project be done in parts or steps?
• Can the parts or steps be done at different times?

If you answer "yes" to both questions, then consider doing the project over a period of time, rather than all at once. (This idea is discussed in detail on the next page.).

Go on an Information Diet

Have you ever taken a week's vacation in an isolated place— somewhere with no real access to phones, faxes, or newspapers? When you returned after having been out of the loop for a whole week, were you at a loss or did you feel renewed and relaxed?

You can reclaim the feeling of renewal when you choose to go on an information diet. Choose information that supports your interests and goals in life, rather than the random barrage that assaults you at work, over the airways, and in print. Take a break—don't buy a Sunday newspaper, turn off the evening news, practice switching off and tuning out. Try going a whole day without turning on the computer or watching television, and see if you feel like you've had a vacation.

Alternately, if being a recluse doesn't appeal to you, try collecting things of interest to you in a journal, notebook, shoebox, or scrapbook. Become actively engaged in learning about something that captures your imagination or interest. This process will revitalize the spirit of learning in age glutted with information.

Create Transitions between Work and Vacation

In his book *Breathing Space,* author Jeff Davidson asks you to review the last time you went away on a refreshing, stress-free vacation full of clear air, relaxing thoughts, and new explorations. Did the benefits of the trip disappear the first day back to your desk where you had to ascend paper mountains, ford a stream of phone messages, and strive to keep your head above the quick sand which had swallowed up your desk?

Davidson suggests avoiding this jarring effect by planning how you ease into vacation and back into work. Don't overplan what you'll try to get done on the day before you go. When you come back plan on taking one day to land at home and get situated. Review your calendar before going, including what happens before, during, and after the vacation. Write yourself a "welcome back" note and take a moment to clean your desk before leaving. Then try to go back to work after the busiest part of the week—Wednesday, Thursday, Friday. Create transitions that bridge the experience of work and vacation.

5. Other tips for thinking creatively about spare moments

Since we have lost the pausing moment in today's sped-up life, reconfigure how you think about certain imposed moments. Consider how you might reuse that time to enjoy something you never have the time for.

Think transportability.

What simple leisure activities can you enjoy just about anywhere?
 • List something you could do on a coffee break or in a traffic jam.

_____

Just say no to time abuse. Use your moments.

Suppose you could buy a packet of "fifteen minutes free time" each day.
 • List what you'd enjoy doing with that extra fifteen minutes (read, garden, practice drawing, etc.).

_____

 • List something you could change in your life in order to get an extra fifteen minutes each day.

_____

The Wise Use of Small Leisure Moments

Many leisure and recreation specialists point out that we are often preoccupied with acquiring large chunks of time, especially in the form of extended holidays and vacations. These large chunks take the most planning and often require the greatest financial investment.

Unfortunately, this preoccupation distracts us from quality experiences found in the often-neglected *brief* leisure moments. These moments may consist of nothing more than taking a mid-morning

coffee break, strolling instead of shopping, climbing stairs instead
of taking the elevator, or gazing out your window at work or
while caught in a traffic jam. In fact, commuting may take on a
whole new look when you begin to examine how you can use
those "dead" moments spent in slowly moving vehicles. Consider
the example of a Los Angeles reporter describing commuters who
bring their leisure activities along for the ride. In the middle of
traffic jams people were reading, playing the violin, meditating,
writing, and singing. Personally, I carry my blues tapes and harmonica. I make quite a sight in the middle of a traffic jam!

While some things—such as putting in a garden, building a
deck, or remodeling—can only be accomplished with large
amounts of time, even these tasks can be broken down into smaller,
doable tasks which can then be slipped in and out of your schedule as time permits. Each of the smaller pieces can be manipu-
lated like cards in a deck that you shuffle and reshuffle to meet
your time options.

The home remodeling project, for example, consists of a series
of semiautonomous tasks: removing old wallpaper, looking at
color samples, painting, reading about floor installation, installing
the floor, researching loans, reading about electrical wiring or getting a demonstration, networking to find a helper or guide, etc.
Create a list of all the tasks and the estimated time for each. Then
consult this list whenever you feel a spare moment or break in
your normal routine coming on. Pick a task that matches your
level of energy or enthusiasm at the moment. Weaving the many
tasks into available moments may result in the entire project
becoming something you look forward to each week. You may
even miss it when you are finally sitting in that newly remodeled
den, reading a favorite magazine and listening to Mozart.

Concluding Thoughts about Time

Many people have described aspects of life in the twentieth century with terms like "lost generation," "future shock," "other-
directed," or "transitional." These different images all share one

image in common: that of a people experiencing profound identity crisis.

Some people today suggest that this search for meaning and identity has resulted from having too many choices, rather than too few. Instead of becoming a gateway to freedom, our wealth of options tether us to a dilemma. And this conundrum echoes through our leisure and free time experiences.

In the end, you may come to realize that the inquiry into the increase or decrease of leisure time is really a superficial question. We each have a certain amount of time in our lives, and much of that time is already spoken for. Still, if you focus on *quality* rather than *quantity* you'll come to realize that the most important change you can make is in your attitude toward the time you have right now.

CHAPTER 3

In the Beginning, the Word Was Play

N THIS CHAPTER, we will examine the evolving nature of our leisure ethic, the connection between work and leisure, and some of the current problems and future choices facing us.

The definition or status of leisure has constantly changed throughout time and from culture to culture. When the ancient Greeks spoke of their leisure, they used the word *schole*, which means "to learn" or "becoming enlightened" (and later became our root word for "school"). Romans, on the other hand, used the Latin word *licere*, emphasizing choice or "to be permitted." And the modern-day French concentrate on the notion of unobligated time when they use the word *loisir* to denote "free time."

Leisurely Words and Ethics

If you could travel back in time to visit a Neolithic band of hunters and gathers, you might find them decorating spears with ritualistic carvings. Hoping to endow the spear with special powers, they sing or chant as they work. Life in the Stone Age was a fusion of many experiences—hunting and gathering, rituals and religions, work and play, all equally valued.

Our progenitors were not chained to an eight hour hunting day, forty hours a week; they spent far more time in ritual and celebration than we do today. Perhaps this is the source of our long-standing fascination with earlier societies. Though we have described these cultures with words like "primitive," they offer the urban dwellers of the late twentieth century a valuable lesson in the art of playful work. They engaged in a meaningful form of labor, as opposed to ours, which tends to be alienating. I believe that many of us, in fact, yearn for a return to this earlier cultural ethos where work and play were in greater balance. Certainly, others have had similar ideas. Confucius, for example, advised that if you choose a job you love, you will never have to work a day in your life.

Now, travel on a bit in time to the roots of Western civilization, planted in Greece and Crete. Here you will see leisure valued and acknowledged with words, and celebrated in deeds. Peoples in these cultures believed that one's highest potential was to be discovered during leisure rather than work hours. The Greeks believed that one's personal development was best explored through fitness (sports), learning (philosophy and science), and creative expression (poetry, drama, pottery). According to leisure wellness author Dr. C. Forrest McDowell, Plato asserted, "You learn more about a person in an hour of play than a lifetime of conversation."

Many early civilizations spent a great deal of time celebrating life. According to Witold Rybczynski, author of *Waiting for the Weekend,* the Egyptians had seventy holidays, the Athenians attended fifty to sixty annual festivals, and the fun-loving Romans indulged in 175 annual public holidays.

Even medieval peasants, who lived under harsh conditions in the so-called dark ages, often were able to spend more than half their waking hours away from work. This is markedly different from conditions in the modern industrial world, where unions had to fight to get the workweek reduced to forty hours. Today, after well over two thousand years of recorded history, most of us are obligated to spend more than half our waking hours at work.

In more recent history, several twentieth-century nations have tried to control or manipulate their citizens' leisure. The Nazis, for instance, attempted to provide the "right kind" of free time by distributing free tickets for approved social events: theater, opera, concerts, resorts, cruises (while also trying to promote tourism and spending as well).

Other countries, including Portugal, Spain, and Italy, at one time had state-run leisure organizations. Citizens were encouraged to partake in state-sanctioned activities as an expression of patriotic duty. The program fit into an overall economic stimulus plan, where state-offered discounts became the inducement. In all of the above cases, the state worked against the grain, trying to turn the highly personal nature of leisure into a collective propaganda or social engineering enterprise.

Work Triumphs over Leisure

Despite this long tradition of integrating and emphasizing leisure, Western civilization ended up saddled with a work ethic that often overpowers our basic need to recreate and relax in equal measure to our labor. The conquest of the leisure ethic by the work ethic can be traced to the rise of the industrial era and the subsequent values expressed by newly emerging cultures.

The rise of the work ethic went hand-in-hand with Puritan notions that idleness (or leisure) was the devil's workshop. They believed that one obtained salvation only through (good) work, and through these beliefs, managed to drive Western civilization in a direction 180 degrees from its Athenian and Cretan roots. By the nineteenth century, most westerners accepted the notion that one's fullest potential could only be achieved through meaningful work.

Harvey Mindness, psychiatrist and comedian, considers how these anti-play and anti-humor attitudes stifle healthy outlooks. He greets humor and playfulness as a divine interruption in an everyday routine and, further, notes that most jokes ridicule or make light of our sexual mores and rituals, authority figures (teachers, parents, religious leaders), work, and the body politic. Naturally, this sort of comedic assault threatens people who believe that most social ills can be traced to too much free time and irreverent laughter. Johan Huizinga, author of *Homo Ludens* (Man at Play), takes the analysis deeper, suggesting that play (like chaos) is older and more original than civilization itself.

As a result, many of us have inherited a guilt that impedes our pursuit of healthy leisure. Free moments become equated with laziness and selfishness. Consider what you do when you arrive home a bit early from work. Does that extra time conjure up a feeling of uneasiness, does your to-do list tug at your sleeve? Do you find yourself trying to get a jump on your obligations by choosing to fill that spare moment with a chore? Or, like so many people, you may be more comfortable doing work or chores— rather than enjoying your leisure options.

New discoveries by biologists illustrate the aberrant nature of this triumph of work over leisure. Zoologist Joan Herbers kept a close record of how animals, including monkeys, rabbits, and various insects, spent their time. She found that chimps used most of their time in grooming, strolling, or just sprawling about, and that even the busy bees and ants spent most of their days inactive. All the animals she studied appeared to carry out chores and complete necessary survival tasks as the opportunity or urge arose, and spent about 50 to 70 percent of their waking time lounging in the sun or sleeping. Work was not the routine, but the break from routine.

In the end, we don't seem to doing as well as birds and bees. And the irony of this phrase is fixed in our very faces, once you realize that humans are one of the few earthly species that can laugh or smile. Maybe, however, we can learn the value of goofing off from our biological kin in the animal kingdom.

What, you may ask, does modern man or woman have to smile about anyway? From what we've just seen, yesterday's societies appear to have been more adept at integrating work and leisure than today's sophisticated culture, in which we are literally working ourselves to death.

Symptoms of the Triumph of Work

As the twentieth century draws to a close, the triumph of the work ethic over leisure is nearly complete. The signs or symptoms of this conquest are all about us. As an editor in a publishing house once observed to me, "I never thought that I would be working this hard at my age for more than a few days a month."

The first symptom of the work ethic's triumph expresses itself in a certain loss of innocence most dramatically evident in the debasement of the word *play* ... it's just "kid stuff" after all. Adults rarely want to be caught dead playing unless they are surrounded by children.

As the quality and quantity of play is diminished, we begin to feel that our lives are out of sync with our personal needs. We have come to define a grown-up as someone who accepts the obligation of living to work—rather than working to play. Various attempts at reviving the spirit of playfulness—"new games" in the 1970s and the interest in bringing more humor into the workplace during the 1980s and 1990s—testify to the deep need to rediscover the art of play.

Without play, both work and leisure become impoverished. There is statistical evidence to support this conclusion, evidence that I refer to as the statistics of work/leisure misery. Studies of job and leisure satisfaction reveal that many of us are unhappy with most of what we do in either sphere and that, in fact, for many people, their work will eventually cause illness or even death.

In Japan, some ten thousand executives die each year from *karoshi,* the term for a sudden death brought on by overwork. Their corporations appear to consider it part of the cost of doing business, and compensate the widows accordingly. In America, 52 percent of executives can expect to die of such stress related conditions as heart attacks and strokes. While most executive positions are still held by men, who are historically more prone to such ailments, as women enter the workforce in increasing numbers, they too are rewarded with increasing rates of heart attacks.

Consider how often people voluntarily change jobs. Prior to the loss of many high-paying jobs in the 1980s and 1990s, over 50 percent of the workforce typically changed jobs *voluntarily* every five years during stable or prosperous times. And when questioned, 30 percent believed that their job was bad for their health. They did not always leave the job for opportunity; sometimes, they fled an illness.

At the same time, we were spending between 77 and 100 billion dollars each year on leisure. Yet, half of those surveyed will tell you that their leisure is unsatisfying. Almost every study shows that at least 50 percent of the people polled are unhappy with either their work or leisure—or both.

The second great symptom of the triumph of work over leisure shows up in the process whereby we define our total existence in terms of occupational roles. At a party, people will ask, "So, what do you do?" The overwhelming majority of people reply with their job title: "I'm a teacher (police officer, office manager, retail clerk, carpenter, social worker, etc.)." We believe that we are our job titles! This explains why so many people describe unemployment or retirement as an entrance into the void.

In taking such a one-dimensional view of ourselves, limiting our identity to an occupational title, we end up expecting too much from our jobs. Johnson O'Connor, one of the pioneers of modern vocational aptitude testing, recognized this problem early in the twentieth century. He contended that the average person has three to five strong aptitudes, but is asked to use only one or two of them at work. O'Connor went on to speculate that, "the aptitudes we have and don't use generate a tremendous amount of restlessness or unhappiness." Work alone simply can't challenge us enough; it cannot engage our total being.

A third symptom shows up in the way we experience our leisure, especially the vacations and long weekends. All year long, Gus would sit at the lunch table in the machine shop and talk about his two-week vacation, describing his family's annual trip to the lake in great detail. And each year he would leave with a grin and return with his familiar sardonic smile. "How'd it go, Gus?" He would sit up, look over his sandwich, and say, "I'm just glad to get back. After packing all night, traveling with the brats, fishing five lakes in seven days, I was glad to get back. I spent the rest of my time off at the Gin Mill."

One woman took up bicycling to relax, and ended up experiencing a whole new realm of stress as she tried to set new personal bests each weekend. The workaholic syndrome erodes people's abilities to function outside the work environment. Workaholism is the updated version of the Protestant work ethic.

Altogether too many people view their vacation in the same frame of mind as work, seeing it as a time of conquest. They work at their play, in other words, traveling to six European cities in eight days, visiting mall after mall, going to see every relative possible. Almost makes you glad to get back to work. But, then, maybe you never really left work because the vacation simply became another thing on your to-do list.

This is where some advocates of leisure wellness make an entrance, with a simple message: Your career is basically the sum of two things, work and leisure, and you should search for opportunities to use your talents in *both* spheres. Leisure wellness, in part, is about finding a more balanced view of work and leisure.

Reintegrating Work and Leisure

Hopefully, we know by now that celebrating either work or leisure to the exclusion of the other leads to an undesirable outcome— either slothfulness or workaholism.

And yet, when you think about it, both meaningful work *and* meaningful play are essential to one's well-being. It's always satisfying to use one's talents productively and, what's more, such experiences form the foundation of healthy self-esteem, of being appreciated for who we are and what we can do.

Indeed, one might not be overly dramatic in concluding that society's salvation or renewal lies, in some part, in the reintegration of our work and play lives.

The Work-Leisure Connection

The search for a new direction is complicated by the conflict between our work and leisure values. This struggle is epitomized by the alienated modern laborer who only feels fully human away from the workplace. Tragically, we have become the opposite of what we started out to be. Human evolution began as the story of human ingenuity expressed through the labors of our species, but these days we use our ingenuity in a flight from our labors.

Fortunately, a subtle shift is taking place in the minds of the workers who will live out their careers in the twenty-first century. The twentysomething generation are turning out to be a "new breed" of worker, one that will redefine what's important in a job.

This new breed is not cut from the same cloth as the older, hard-charging baby boom generation. They reject the seventy-hour workweek and hold the work-free weekend as sacred. Twentysomethings value job satisfaction and leisure options over cash as their measure of success. They opt for part-time and temporary positions in order to pursue travels, artistic endeavors, or child rearing. They might choose to go a month without pay in order to realize dreams of travel. Often, they pick a job because of its proximity to their friends, community, or leisure interests. And many are investigating flextime and job sharing in an effort to balance their work life with other parts of their life.

The new breed of workers are not placing their personal lives on hold while they pursue career success. They do not feel obliged to swear loyalty to companies and agencies which no longer offer decent wages or job security. As a result, *Fortune* magazine advises managers to consider more flexible work arrangements if they want to attract the dwindling numbers of young workers.

Seeing a labor market with little promise, this new class of workers shift gears. These pioneers are redefining our work ethic—and not a moment too soon.

In addition, many "older breed" employees, upon reaching midlife, find the workplace growing empty or accelerating at an unhealthy pace for them. The quest for upward mobility loses appeal when you reach a plateau. Amy Salzman has written an entire book, *Downshifting,* about people heading in the opposite direction. These people are opting to withdraw from the materialistic quest for glamour and status—leaving behind a marathon rat race in which only the rats find fulfillment.

As workers change direction, other institutions will be similarly effected. Schools, and especially colleges, will need to redefine their career-education curriculums. For instance, Patsy B. Edwards, one of America's leading pioneers in leisure counseling, suggests a practical way to blend work and leisure counseling. She and Paul Bloland argue that colleges should integrate leisure guidance into their career counseling centers. This idea—a career center catering to both work and leisure ethics—is just one example of the five ways work and leisure tend to be connected.

The Five Connections

In the first connection, many of us first discover our vocational aptitudes through our leisure pursuits. Many people have turned a hobby or volunteer work in computer programming, jewelry making, writing, car repair, child care, or cooking into a business or profession.

In the second connection, people often reach a point in life where the necessity or opportunity to change jobs presents itself. After midlife, this sort of change becomes more complicated; a worker may feel his or her job has grown empty or unrewarding, but may find it difficult to change careers, or even jobs, due to family obligations, medical insurance, pensions, vacation time, or salary. Ironically, this sense of being frozen in a career comes at the moment when one most needs a change.

In such cases, a less dramatic change might be advised. If it seems impossible to make changes in the first eight hours of work, you can always look into making smaller changes in a different eight hours, outside of work. New leisure activities enable you to rejuvenate family bonds, change your surroundings, and spend fun time with people very different from your coworkers.

Leisure gives you a chance to replace worn-out goals with new ones. It allows you to, for instance, discover a new passion, in pursuing that old dream of a mountain cabin, turning a hobby into a "second career," performing in a local musical group, or joining a social or civic group. Often, this new enthusiasm can carry over and reinvigorate your work life.

Leisure also offers many more options than the labor market. While you may have, on the average, one to thirteen different jobs throughout your life, you can try out an unlimited number of leisure activities. Begin with doing absolutely nothing, and stretch to bungie-cord jumping, growing a vegetable garden, or collecting antiques. Whatever you like!

In the third connection, we find that work productivity depends on play activity. Witold Rybczynski, author of *Waiting for the Weekend,* reports that England and the Soviet Union tried to shorten their workers' weekend, with disastrous results. When the weekend was shortened in favor of a longer workweek, output dropped as people began taking Mondays off or working less strenuously. The lesson to be learned is that output may be not only a product of how long one works, but also of how long one has for recreation and leisure.

It is also important to note the crucial role that a person's attitude plays in recovery and longevity. A study released in 1994 showed that people with an altruistic attitude often survive heart problems in far better health, and subsequently live longer, than those with pessimistic outlooks. In fact, people with relatively minor heart conditions and negative outlooks did less well than those with more severe conditions and positive outlooks. Feelings of anger, anxiety, insecurity, doubt, and pessimism generally lead people to the grave earlier than their medical conditions alone. You need to examine your day-to-day emotional state, personal values or outlook, and connection with others, and then ask, "How can I enhance my attitude through my leisure involvement?"

As more and more people see the connection between stress reduction and healthy leisure, even greater benefits are certain to be realized. For instance, anyone who's responsible for employee well-being knows the value of mixing play and work. In a recent survey of human-resource specialists, humor was identified as a key success factor in situations such as discussing a problem with a colleague, conducting a job interview, or relieving tension at a meeting.

Furthermore, business consultant and psychologist Bruce Roselle believes that people who incorporate play in their work come the closest to performing at their peak.

The fourth connection is between job-hunting skills and successful techniques for finding meaningful leisure opportunities. In fact, as you master the less formal leisure-search techniques, you'll improve your job-finding skills as well. In a project I coordinated at Portland State University, graduate students taught high school special-education students how to assess their leisure interests, network to find information about leisure opportunities, and interview experts in a leisure area of interest.

Interestingly, those students who practiced both job and leisure search skills had higher rates of employment than their peers who received no training. In fact, those students who received nine weeks of job-search training and nine weeks of leisure-search training found jobs at the same rate as those student who received eighteen weeks of job-search training. Those receiving the combined search training were also more confident about persisting in their search for work or leisure.

When teachers and career counselors integrate the search for leisure with the search for work, they give students a powerful tool for personal development. Unfortunately, this blending of work and leisure education is only a visionary—and rarely seen—alternative to the standard curriculum. If truth be known, our schools typically provide a second-rate job search education and no leisure education at all. Career education is rarely offered as a stand-alone class, and career centers are one of the first services to be cut during a budget crunch.

When schools *do* experiment with leisure education, it is often relegated to after school, or to programs serving special populations, such as students with developmental disabilities.

Educators and parents assume that students will develop a successful leisure ethic on their own—despite the fact that our culture is often biased against leisure. As a result, many instead succumb to boredom, often with disastrous results. Every day, we are bombarded with stories of young people pursuing unhealthy leisure activities, such as drug abuse or getting involved with gangs. Perhaps it's time to consider moving the topic of leisure into the definition of basic education, just as we have with health.

In the fifth connection, we find leisure transforming itself into a work-alternative. Where once the job was one's primary source of pride, these days a person's greatest source of self-worth may well come from the recognition they get for talents displayed during leisure hours.

Without knowing it, we may be returning to the ancient Greeks' outlook, moving towards a scenario in which people find their greatest worth and interest concentrated in their leisure hours. Some people argue that this is because so many "job skills" are now embedded in a computer chip, leaving a preponderance of dumbed-down jobs in the service sector—jobs that consist of hitting the correct button on a keypad and saying "have a nice day" to the customer. Witold Rybczynski summed it up this way: The weekend has become the last opportunity not to escape work but rather to create work that is meaningful in order to realize the satisfaction that is no longer afforded in the workplace.

Attempting to Define Leisure

Let us end this examination of the evolution of work and play by returning to the challenge of defining leisure. As I see it, leisure has five essential qualities:

1. It is something that involves personal choice. You determine (within the confines of your lifestyle) when, where, and what you'll do.

2. Leisure experiences give back energy, renew, or relax you.

3. Leisure should not destroy mental or physical health.

4. Leisure gives you fulfillment, meaning, or satisfaction.

5. Healthy leisure embodies a spirit of playfulness.

Instead of offering a precise list of criteria, these five qualities can be used to gauge and examine your own leisure experiences. Remember that the leisure experience is not defined by what you *do,* but by your attitude. The way you approach a particular activity determines if you will find it playful, energizing, and renewing or forced, exhausting, and unhealthy.

Some people face the unusual dilemma of not having a clear dividing line between their work and play. This is especially true for creative workers and professionals, such as artists, writers, athletes, designers, consultants, and certain types of self-employed skilled and managerial workers. Because their work is also their play these "workers" may become isolated by their single-minded passions and pursuits.

For example, when an artist spends a great deal of time crafting his or her art, then the search for leisure wellness shifts targets. Instead of looking for an activity that fully engages their passions and thoughts, the artists' task is to find a balance between work and other uses of time. They have to learn to leave behind their creative work in order to participate in leisure experiences which renew and refresh.

In addition, their work is often isolating. Therefore, they face the additional challenge of developing leisure interests which have a socializing content. They are well advised to avoid spending all of their time planning—like the marathon runner, who in the end crosses the finish line alone.

Knowing that our lives are compressed and hurried, you will find it helpful to enjoy a leisurely pause—away from this book. It is time to stop and digest the information and opinions expressed so far. Take a break from the book, perhaps a few hours or a few days. Ponder how leisure has changed, examine the changes you have seen in your lifetime. Discuss your ideas with others. When you return, this reflective pause will be extended in the form of a journal writing assignment that provides an opportunity to ponder your attitude towards leisure and work. You will be asked to take these reflective pauses throughout this book. Hopefully, this process will provide you with the necessary time to capture and record your evolving leisure ethic.

Exercise 6:
Leisure Journal Assignment: Summing Up

As in all journal writing, what matters at this point is the process and not the literary product. That is, you are writing to an audience of one: YOU. Therefore, the best type of writing is the style that comes from the heart and honestly reflects your feelings and thoughts, your doubts and questions. Don't worry about punctuation or grammar. Once you gather your thoughts, write quickly. Keep your hand moving and get out your ideas—or you will find self-criticism and editing creeping into your writing. When that happens, the writing will stop or become labored.

  1. List three important ways in which leisure has changed from early society to the present. Choose three ideas that seem to reflect some aspect of your own leisure life.

_____

_____

_____

  2. Which of the several work-leisure connections discussed above do you find most meaningful?

_____

_____

_____

Defining Leisure Wellness

Defining leisure wellness is simpler than defining leisure itself, because we are modifying the broader word "leisure" with the more specific term "wellness." This helps to narrow down the discussion. So, from here on, the task of defining leisure is left to the reader, as our focus shifts to wellness.

The wellness movement has always stressed taking responsibility for one's own health, and emphasized avoiding the sorts of sickness that result from neglect. Wellness advocates advise their followers to stop depending on others (doctors) to make them healthy. Similarly, *leisure* wellness leaders would remind you of the title of Patsy Edward's book, *You've Got to Go Find Happiness, It Won't Find You.*

You can take your first step towards healthy leisure by trying to adopt a more playful attitude at work. The "humor in the workplace" movement that began in earnest in the 1980s is a trend in this healthy direction. Perhaps you could begin the next committee meeting with a short magic trick, cartoon, joke, or story. Another way to become more playful would be to get more involved in social events or join with co-workers on community service projects. These activities can extend your job description, build a sense of community, and add depth to your work experience.

Author Steve Wilson provides many practical suggestions for incorporating humor and playfulness at work. Here is a summary of his and other people's suggestions:

- Replace coffee breaks with joke-telling breaks. Ask people to submit jokes for certain days of the week.
- Show a video at lunch, and serve popcorn.
- Make a humorous employee-orientation tape for new employees, showing what people "really" do on the job.
- Bring in a massage therapist for fifteen-minute breaks.
- Bring in a Polaroid or caricaturist to capture people at a meeting. Ask people to suggest captions for the pictures.
- Develop a wastebasket free-throw contest.
- Organize a day of community service or a school partnership project.

- Organize "dress-up days," with themes like the 1950s, or Star Trek. Alternately, ask people to wear clothes they wear while enjoying leisure or hobbies.
- Develop opportunities for people to display or share their hobbies and leisure interests.
- Match baby pictures or high school yearbook photos to current staff.
- Organize a once-a-week dinner, book, or movie club.
- Bring your child, spouse (or partner or friend) to work.
- Put a stack of ten one-dollar bills in the middle of a table when brainstorming. Give a dollar each to the first ten people to come up with ideas.
- Put a humor program on the computer for a day. Place funny calendars by the copy machine.
- Put together a leisure club, in which a group of people complete this book together and then go on a leisure search (described in later chapters).

Leisure and play do have a cost. These ideas will remain simply a list unless someone is appointed to coordinate or encourage these events. Perhaps once a month, an employee could be relieved for a few hours a week to set up and coordinate the selected healthy leisure events.

Often, one needs to search for leisure wellness outside the workplace. As already noted, this is especially true when you feel you have reached a career plateau. At this point, you can search for appreciation, recognition, and a sense of accomplishment in your leisure pursuits. It might mean training for a marathon, helping in the Big Brothers or Big Sisters organizations, working in a food bank, growing a vegetable or flower garden, trying out for local drama or dance productions, and so on.

One piece of advice: Leisure wellness should not result in changing an addiction to work into an addiction to a specific form of play. Carefully examine your use of leisure time. Do you always have your nose in a book? Are you watching too much television?

Are you spending every spare moment at the gym? Make sure that your intense devotion has not shut the world out the way a drug numbs you to outside realities.

Learning from Those Who Have Retired from Their First Careers

In this book, retirement will be referred to as one's second career, and will be discussed more fully in the next chapter.

In 1900, the average American's life expectancy was forty-seven; by the end of the century it will be ninety. With this tremendous increase in longevity, one can begin to speak of a second career beginning as you exit your first career. Unfortunately, many retired people will face another twenty to thirty years of vitality burdened by the terms "senior citizen" or "retiree."

Most retirees underestimate the amount of free time they could have at their disposal each day: a whopping thirteen hours of discretionary time (after subtracting seven hours for sleep and four hours for chores)! When you don't plan for this kind of change in lifestyle, the results can be devastating. It has been reported that people who retire without a plan receive an average of thirteen checks from social security before dying.

Regardless of your age, there are lessons to learn from the experience of those who have retired and adjusted successfully. The basic one is: don't leave leisure planning until after retirement! Rather, you must try to integrate leisure into your life as soon as possible. Tomorrow may come too quickly. If you've paid your dues during your first career, don't neglect to plan for the harvest in your second career.

Leisure Wellness Begins When You Develop a Plan

If you talk to those wise people who are enjoying their second careers, you will soon see the value of developing a plan for your own second career. Such a plan must be built upon a solid understanding of your leisure interests, preferences, and talents. And you will have this understanding after completing the leisure inventories found throughout the rest of this book.

As you become more excited about the possibilities, your plan will become part of a deeply felt passion for the design or purpose of your life. It should be similar to the plan you may have developed for your occupational career early in life. Planning for your leisure will help balance the equation. The final chapter will help you write and visualize this plan.

The following journal exercise is a prelude to some deeper thinking about your leisure preferences and interests.

Exercise 7:
Leisure Journal Assignment: Environmental Scan

In this three-part exercise, you will scan your environment for clues about your personal preferences, styles, and interests.

Step 1: The Floor Plan

On another piece of paper draw a basic floor plan for your house, showing the approximate location of rooms in relationship to one another. You should include garages, basements, or second stories in a second block.

Stare at the drawing for a bit, and then pick out the three rooms or places where you most enjoy spending time, according to these criteria:

- One room for sleeping or resting (bedroom, lounge, living room, study, etc.)
- One storage or work place (attic, garage, art room, office, etc.)
- One room for entertaining or meeting (family room, kitchen, dining room, game room, etc.)

Step 2: Environmental Scan

Now actually visit each room. But do it as if you had never been there before, like an alien visitor or a private investigator looking for clues about the inhabitants. As you scan each room look for clues about how the inhabitant (you) spends his or her leisure time. Look for any clue, no matter how big or how small. Below your drawing, list the clues you find.

Analyze your environmental scan data by asking the following questions:

1. How many of the clues describe activities that are done by yourself alone, and how many with others, or simply around others?

2. Which activities represent things you enjoyed as a child or young adult?

3. Which activities are done out of habit or are less than satisfying?

4. Which ones do you enjoy the most?

Step 3: Definition of Leisure

Based on this data, write your new definition of leisure and wellness or healthy leisure.

CHAPTER 4

Starting Your Second Career after Retirement

F ANY OF the following statements describe your present situation, then this chapter was written for you:

- You have put off thinking about your leisure because you're too busy and think you can tackle that question after you retire.

- You are approaching retirement.

- You have retired and are searching for a meaningful use of your free time

- You work with older citizens and want to become more fully aware of the leisure issues they face.

Stages and Phases of the Second Career

Your life can be pictured as a series of age stages: childhood, adolescence, young adulthood, midlife, and senior. Potentially, the longest period will be spent in those last two stages.

The midlife period, which starts at age thirty or thirty-five, extends some thirty years and is generally is seen as the most productive of life's stages. It represents the culmination or peak in one's (first) career. The subsequent senior years, which may also extend some thirty or more years, are then viewed as the "retirement" stage.

Given our increased longevity and vitality, the word *retirement* needs to undergo a metamorphosis, to be reconnected with the notion of career. Currently, the word has many negative connotations, as evidenced by the synonyms listed for it in a thesaurus: departure, resignation, withdrawal, solitude, resignation, termination. All of these words describe an exit. We have few words to describe the new potentials that, these days, begin to appear around the age of sixty or sixty-five.

As I see it, retirement is not an exit, but an entrance. It can become a career juncture, a transition point leaving behind one form of work and pursuing another. Perhaps you'll shift from working for others to working for yourself. Maybe you'll want to turn a hobby into a business. If you've tried several different occupations (full or part time) it may be time to simplify your worklife. On the other hand, you may want to go from full-time to part-time or temporary status. Others will want to concentrate on volunteer work or a hobby.

Redefining Work in the Second Career

One normally chooses a first career based on one's education and the need to support oneself (and often others). However, one's choice of a "second career" (as I will refer to retirement from here on) will probably be based more on accumulated wisdom and experience, together with more consideration of the purpose or mission of one's own life.

It helps to remember that the word "career" originally referred to a course or pathway. Unlike those alternate words for retirement considered above, the word *career* has many ennobling synonyms: history, calling, avocation, profession, livelihood, pursuits, specialty, experience. It includes what you do for pay, for free, and for yourself. Leisure values (and your view of leisure time) play a critical part in setting the direction of your second career. Indeed, your second career choice may be your most important career choice.

By linking the concepts of "retirement" and "career" we expand the possibilities. Regardless of one's age, there are still many

"You'll be in good shape if you don't live too long."

© 1992 Tribune Media Services. Reprinted with permission.

adventures, risks, and learning experiences ahead. Whether you are graduating from school or leaving your job, any change in "career" will be fraught with fears and hopes. Looking at it this way, retirement could simply mark a graduation from your first career to your second.

In an AARP (American Association of Retired Persons) article about opportunities during the senior stage, Charles Hand suggests thinking about the second career as a time to cash in on one's portfolio of talents. He urges the reader to "... do some things for money, some because they interest you, some out of love or kindness, and some for the sheer hell of it." In this fashion, one expands the meaning of the word "work" to include all the activities in which you use your talents, paid or otherwise.

Mr. Hand further observes that as organizations slim down there will be fewer permanent full-time positions and a far larger need for temporary specialists. This leads to the sort of temporary arrangement that could be very appealing to people just retiring from their first career. Hand predicts that in the near future

20 percent of employees at many companies will be full time, and 80 percent will come and go.

Phases in the Second Career

Unfortunately, the later stages of life are generally lumped together under the label "senior citizen." By contrast, Elwood Chapman, who has written extensively about retirement and career planning, describes several seasons of growth and change which stretch across one's later years. I have adopted his model to describe four basic phases, with an emphasis on leisure options.

Each phase has its own set of roles, challenges, and tasks. In the next exercise, you'll read about each phase, and then decide which one comes closest to describing your present situation. Each description includes suggested strategies for enhancing your experience and successfully negotiating its challenges.

Exercise 8:
Second Career Phase Inventory

Identify the phase that best describes you, then underline a strategy which sounds helpful to you in this phase. (Don't be afraid to borrow any strategy at any stage.) If the following description of phases or cycles does not speak to you, then pull ideas from this activity and invent a description that best describes the phase you feel you are in at this point and write it down in the space provided at the end.

Phase 1: The Graduating "Senior"

Description:
This is a period of adjustment in which you throw off your previous main responsibility (work). From now on, "work" may be performed for pay outside the home or inside the home (typically without pay). The old sources of your identity and satisfaction, rooted in your first-career role, have disappeared. You must anticipate traveling an arduous path as you grope for a new direction in life.

The main task or challenge:
To accept that your first career is over and a new one has begun. Your goal is to carve out a new identity, a new dream, a new goal.

Coping strategies:
1. Begin with a vacation or change of routine as a rite of passage to a larger life-change (cruise, trip to a resort or to visit relatives, or many short trips).

2. Keep a journal

3. Ask other people to finish the phrase, "When I retire, I've always wanted to. . . ." Compile a list of suggestions. When you've heard from others, and gotten a feeling for the kinds of lists people make, begin adding your own suggestions as they occur to you.

4. Write up a short-term plan, listing things to investigate.

5. If you are feeling uneasy, depressed, angry, withdrawn, fixated on your health, or empty you may wish to seek professional help.

Phase 2: The Action Years

Description:
This phase is full of action and energy as you spread your wings, take risks, pursue lifelong dreams, and create new dreams. You might explore one or several new adventures including: traveling, seasonal or part-time work, starting a business, volunteering, consulting, and exploring leisure pursuits. When you feel you've started moving toward your new goals, toward fulfilling a long term dream or passion, then you're ready for the next phase. One caution, however: Don't move into the next phase simply because you failed to discover a passion or a new dream.

The main task or challenge:
To find that dream—a new source of joy, some kind of goal which ignites your passions or speaks to your soul.

Strategies for exploring possible goals:

1. Examine your leisure interests using the exercises in this book. Examine your values and preferences. Consider taking an aptitude, personality, or values test to discover some of the "drivers" in your life. You may want to talk to a career or general-purpose counselor and take tests such as a Meyers-Briggs, or enroll in the nonprofit Johnson O'Connor testing centers. There are also many self-help books and classes out there that can help you assess your values, aptitudes, and interests. Don't neglect advice from friends and other helpers, such as religious leaders.

2. Become more eccentric, speak out more, be adventuresome. Taking some new risks can help you break out of self-imposed limits.

3. Laugh more. Study humor and magic.

4. Change your appearance or wardrobe to reflect a new image, a new start in life.

5. Start new exercise or diet programs.

Phase 3: The Mellow Years

Description:
This phase is less active, but it allows for more balance and may, therefore, be more precious. It is time to set a new course and slow the pace a bit. It is a mellowing phase, a time to think of yourself first and reduce external demands and pressures.

The main task or challenge:
To find the balance point between phases 2 and 4. This means deciding what to give up or reduce on your daily menu of activities. It also means exploring new sources of involvement. Self-pacing is the key to finding this balance. Ask yourself questions like: What dream can I still pursue? What am I still curious about? What talents have I yet to explore?"

Strategies for finding a new balance:

1. Decide how you will balance all of the demands on your time. Make an inventory of your current obligations and then prioritize. What things are you doing out of habit? Which things cause too much stress? Which can you still do if you adapt or adjust how you do them?

2. Plan better for high-energy activities and perhaps do fewer. Plan for "recovery days" after days requiring a high expenditure of energy.

3. Let go of relationships and memberships which no longer matter.

4. Try changing your sleep or work cycles. Many people find this is a good time to try "earlier to bed and earlier to rise." However, if you are a night person, try turning your night into day.

5. Start a journal or write your memoirs.

Phase 4: Journey to the Interior

Description:

As the body becomes less active, the mind becomes more involved. In this phase, you become more an observer than a doer, and come to terms with the fact that observing is as joyful as participation. You can find great pleasure in simple activities like viewing sunsets, visiting with friends and family, going out to eat simpler meals, or driving through your community. Television or computers play an increasing role in connecting you with the world. Memories become more important. Your home remains your castle. The rocking chair is finally permitted.

Your contacts with people will be fewer but more enjoyable. There is probably more pill-taking in this phase. Previous standards are even less important and, in fact, eccentricity becomes you in this phase.

People who enjoy this stage often keep their minds moving into a new and exciting sphere of spiritual or secular wisdom.

Thus, while you may feel more comfortable staying in your home, your mind can still travel great distances. You might come to understand the world, the heavens, and your place within the entire scheme of things. You may discover wonder.

The main task or challenge:
Now it is time to come to terms with your own mortality and accept that your course is set. Once you accept this, you will be able to push away from previous fears. This understanding leads to a greater peace and tranquillity. Full acceptance comes when you realize the value of remaining curious. In this way, you can define living as learning.

Strategies for remaining curious:
1. Take pride in your appearance. Dress for all outside activities.
2. Take a trip to your childhood roots.
3. Begin to sum up your life experiences. This can be done in many different ways: redo the family photo albums, write memoirs, keep a journal, collect family recipes, make a video life-story for your grandchildren, distribute possessions, or visit people who can share memories with you.
4. Discuss both your first and second careers with those you love.
5. Laugh more often at your foibles (memory, confusion, mistakes).
6. Enjoy visitors.
7. Show off—use untypical language, spend money recklessly if you feel like it.
8. Examine spiritual writings or speculate about the cosmos on your own.

Try inventing your own phase

If you want to invent a phase that more accurately describes your current situation, fill in the blanks below.

Name of the phase:

_____

Description:

_____

_____

The main task or challenge:

_____

_____

Strategies for success in this phase:

_____

_____

Successful Career-Planning Tips

To be successful in any career, one must try to answer the question you first encountered in childhood: "What do you want to be when you grow up?" The well-kept secret is that all of our lives we are "becoming something," or growing up. This means that what you want to be continually changes; still, the original question remains as a helpful prompt, forcing you to review who you are . . . and what you want to become. In the second career, the question is modified slightly to "What do you want to become now that you are grown up?"

Success in your first career is often measured in terms of occupational achievement or family fortune. Success in the second career depends on a larger mission: a sense of personal fulfillment. To be successful in either career you must prepare, develop a plan, and pursue your dream with vigor. The pursuit energizes your life, and this newfound vitality leads to greater fulfillment.

Examining Your Thoughts about Planning

Before you can start planning for your second career, you must examine your attitude about planning. Ask yourself, "What do I value or believe about the desirability of planning for my second career?" Three common opinions about planning are listed below. Check off the one that comes closest to your experience or belief system.

- I'm waiting until I retire before I pursue any hobbies. Then I'll have plenty of time and energy to get started.
- I was fairly successful in my first career. I don't expect developing a second career will take much.
- I don't need to worry about what to do in my second career. There are plenty of odd jobs waiting for me.

Now complete the following exercise to find alternatives to these planning myths.

Exercise 9:
The Second-Career Planning Riddle

Each person has a different way of answering this riddle. After you develop your response, find out what others think. Ask people who have been successful in their transition to a second career. You will enjoy comparing your answers. Before filling out the next page, copy it so you can show another person.

Assume you are at a graduation party for your young nephew Milford. You ask Milford, "What are your plans now that you're out of school?"

Milford looks around, sighs, shrugs, and then replies, "Oh, I'm going to live at home awhile, look around, and see what comes up."

You probe further, "Don't you have a career plan or goal?"

Milford responds, "Not just yet. Most of my friends can't seem to find a good job. I mean, what's the point? Why do I need a career goal?"

You find this kind of disheartening. What advice will you give Milford? What advice might you offer any young graduate about career planing? Stop for a moment and respond to poor Milford. Write down a few lines of advice.

_____

_____

_____

_____

To varying degrees, almost everyone stresses the need to have some kind of plan. While some talk about the need for specific, measurable goals, others emphasize the importance of simply having a direction. The reasons given are varied: If you take just anything that comes up, you might waste valuable opportunities to explore and try things that really interest you; developing a vision or mission helps give you a sense of purpose; people with goals seem to be more involved with life, happier regardless of their specific missions.

Now imagine that a strange thing happens. Several years have passed and Milford has been working away at a career. It is early spring and Milford has just arrived at your retirement party. Milford, looking wiser for the years, turns to you and asks, "What are your plans?"

You laugh and hear yourself saying, "Milford, it's funny you should ask. I was just going to kick around for a while, sleep in late, take it easy and see what comes." You both laugh at this sublime form of poetic justice.

The final question becomes: Does the advice you originally gave Milford now apply to you? What are your thoughts?

More Information on the
Common Myths about Planning

Each of the statements below is considered a myth for the following reasons:

I'm waiting until I retire before I pursue my hobbies. Then I'll have plenty of time and energy to get started. Few people suddenly develop hobbies after a lifetime without them. Opportunity—or hobbies—rarely come knocking at your door. Instead, it is best to sample several different leisure pursuits well before you retire. Then, when you suddenly find yourself with more time and energy, you'll be ready to take off from the second-career launching pad. Otherwise, you'll be faced with the dilemma of trying to go and discover a new direction or a new hobby during a very confusing life-phase.

I was fairly successful in my first career. I don't expect developing a second career will take much. Success in a first career does not guarantee anything about the second half of life. In fact, people who have adjusted to a very average first career achievement, may do much better than the high achievers. Think about, for example, a bank guard who accepted and even enjoyed his job to a degree. He also cherished his many hobbies which included fishing, gardening, and volunteer work at the local food bank.

This is in sharp contrast with the bank's CEO, who was accustomed to being very successful, very important, and very busy. Suddenly after retirement the CEO found that his advice was not sought after, his special privileges vanished, and he faced an empty calendar. He would have been much better off scheduling a bit of leisure time years before, and finding out what he wanted to really do.

One bank president did just that. She discovered that she liked backpacking, motorcycles, and collecting 1950s memorabilia. After her retirement, she had plenty of things to do. She and her husband went on a cross-country motorcycle trip. Later, she put on greasy overalls and learned to repair her motorcycles. Just like the guard, she found new sources of importance or achievement and involvement.

I don't need to worry about what to do in my second career. There are plenty of odd jobs waiting for me. Guess what! If those odd jobs weren't important to you before retirement, they aren't going to grow any more attractive after you retire.

The Costs of Not Planning for the Second Career

Like so many others, Vito Paparolli (not his real name) put off thinking about his leisure and his retirement. He underestimated the amount of free time he would have, and found it very difficult to fill thirteen hours a day. Every day goes something like this:

> Vito never sets the alarm, hoping that he'll get up later each day, but he still wakes up at his old work time. He sits in bed a while reviewing plans for the day—but this only takes a moment. He calls the dog, smells the coffee, and finally gets up. At breakfast he reads through two large newspapers and grumbles about the decline of civilization.
>
> He secretly hopes that when he looks up at the clock it will be at least ten o'clock. He goes out to his garage to look over things, putters around, but he has no project, so he just reorganizes some drawers and tools and looks over the old junk stored in tattered cardboard boxes.
>
> Finally, his wife asks him to go out and pick up a quart of milk and a chicken—at last, something to do! Returning home, he spends at least two hours eating lunch and watching a soap opera and his favorite game show. He goes out and talks to a neighbor, but when he comes in he is disappointed because it is only three o'clock. Should he watch a golf tournament or not? He watches an old movie instead, then both the local and national news and one more talk show.
>
> Dinner comes and goes in the quiet house. He settles into his favorite chair to read a book for a while, then thumbs through a magazine. He scans the stations but everything's a rerun. Finally it is 9:30. At last he is happy again because it's time for bed. He's made it through another day of retirement.

Vito thought he would blissfully enjoy doing nothing, but nothing is not easy to do. Thinking back about the many hours he spent dreaming of retirement, Vito can't believe he worked so hard to achieve so little. His second career has him chained to boredom.

Boredom can have negative health consequences. In the previous chapter, it was noted that people who didn't plan for their retirement hours live an average of only thirteen months after retirement. Rozanne Faulkner, a recreation therapist, further observes that "sustained boredom can lead the body into emotional and physical breakdown just as easily as sustained stress."

Don't leave planning for your second career until retirement or age sixty-five. Tomorrow may come too soon.

But I Can't ...

We all have reasons why we don't develop plans, why we can't seem to find the key that turns the motor on. Use the next exercise to help analyze your barriers and then choose strategies for overcoming these barriers.

Exercise 10:
Barriers and Success Strategies

We all face barriers that could prevent us from becoming all that we would like to be. The trick is to confront the barriers and develop strategies for overcoming them. To be successful, consider what small changes you could make in your behavior or attitude to help you develop a new outlook and a new pattern for living. Also, acknowledge that some barriers *can't* be overcome. In those cases, accept the barrier and consider how you might adapt. This can mean, for example, substituting a less demanding activity for a high energy one. If you can't go on a three day camping and fishing trip, can you take a day trip? The following list of barriers is followed by suggested strategies for changing one's behavior or attitude to start overcoming them.

Barriers

Below is a list of reasons why people fail to find fulfillment in later years, often as a result of poor (or no) planning for what will happen after one retires from a paid job or after one's children leave home. If any statement is even somewhat true of your life at this time, put a check in the box.

☐ My retirement (or my empty home) has become a void; I feel withdrawn from the world.

☐ I see my retirement (or empty home) as a prison rather than an opportunity.

☐ I don't want to take risks at my age because of all the disappointments in my preretirement years.

☐ To be honest, I really don't feel proud of being this age. I think a lot about the past or mourn the loss of my youth.

☐ I seem to lack a mission, purpose, or dreams. I often feel passionless. I was programmed to reach retirement or raise my family—but then the program stops.

☐ I seem to have a lot of personal problems taking up my time and energy.

☐ Another possible reason I have not made plans, or feel stalled at this point in life, or have become withdrawn, or feel blue is:

_____

_____

Starter Strategies

Now that you've thought about barriers, let's shift to possible solutions or coping strategies. The next part of this exercise will help you identify changes you can make in your attitude or behavior. This process begins once you decide to get more out of life. Next, you'll need to develop a goal and commit yourself to taking a first step. Think of the list below as a brainstorming tool. The trick is to pick a starter strategy that both excites you and lies within your comfort zone. Additionally, it should feel appropriate to the phase you feel you are in at this moment in time. Check off *all* the ideas that seem meaningful, then whittle your list down to the one or two activities that will best help you start off in a new direction.

- Take a test to assess my leisure or work interests.
- Look for a new job, one I might really enjoy.
- Worry less and daydream more.
- Conduct a self-assessment of my life goals and mission. Try to develop a new purpose, or new goals.
- Change my routine.
- Develop a new dream.
- Provide consulting services.
- Become a "helper" in my community.
- Start a new business.
- Travel: visit my childhood neighborhood, take a grandchild or other special person on a trip, or take my special dream trip.
- Become more eccentric, less conventional.
- Take more risks, try to be more adventuresome.
- Speak out, become more assertive.
- Study comedy, humor, or magic.
- Begin a new diet or exercise program.
- Spend more money than I'm used to (but not more than I have).
- Change my reading habits (read more or less).
- Take more leisurely walks.
- Sum up my experiences by writing a journal or memoir, creating a scrapbook, reorganizing old photo albums, or creating a family genealogy.

- Think less about the past and focus more on the phase I am now in.
- Think more about the past, reminisce but without repeating or boring others.
- Renew contacts with old friends.
- Encourage more visits from others.
- Discourage visits from others.
- Quit old groups or memberships.
- Join new groups, clubs, or associations.
- Change my sleep patterns by going to bed earlier (or later).
- Change my appearance: surgically or with cosmetics, a hairpiece, new wardrobe, etc.
- Enjoy and take pride in my age, think of my age and looks as an achievement.
- Dress each day, refuse to live in robes and pajamas.
- Laugh more.
- Complain less.
- Throw a surprise birthday party for myself.
- Play with children more.
- Play with children less.
- Get advice from a counselor or doctor.
- Visit with a religious leader.
- Join a support group (e.g., men's, women's, widows', adult children of ...).
- Get expert advice about careers, schooling, finances, wellness, or residential options.
- Give away prize possessions to others who will appreciate them.
- Increase my mental activity as my physical abilities decline.

- Become less a doer and more an observer.
- Pay my "rent" on the planet by making some kind of contribution.
- Donate to a charity.
- Write a will or last instructions.
- Hold a family meeting.
- Cook for friends.

Learning to Be Flexible

As noted in the preface, British playwright George Bernard Shaw wisely wrote words to this effect: We do not stop playing because we grow old, we grow old because we stop playing.

Most people probably decrease their play time not because their body grows inflexible, but because their attitude grows rigid. It might sound like, "I don't like to ... I don't want to ... Why should I try? ... What good would it do me? ... I've never done it before ... "

On July 9, 1993 the television show "20/20" reported that, in a study of active, healthy people who had reached the age of 100 (or more), researchers found that their subjects had four things in common. Diet and genetics were not the determining characteristics—acceptance of loss, engagement with life, positive attitude, and flexibility were.

When you are more open to different options, you increase the likelihood of finding something that will engage you (the second longevity factor). If you tend towards inflexibility, or feel that your leisure options are too limited, then try the next exercise.

Exercise 11:
Leisure Flexibility Exercise

Our lives often change dramatically in unexpected ways. These changes may force us to adapt old leisure interests or to explore new options. This exercise will help you to develop a flexible mental attitude toward future leisure options.

Sampler of Leisure Activities

The following is a list of forty examples covering a wide range of leisure activities. You'll be examining this list and your attitudes towards the activities in five steps, and (as with all exercises in this book) the degree to which you are honest with yourself will determine the degree of usefulness of this survey. In the first step you'll fill out the L/D column, in the second step the G, and so on. The directions for each step are found at the end of this list. To begin, skip ahead to those directions, to learn how to complete the L/D column. Do each step, one at a time.

L/D G/S M/F O

1. ☐ ☐ ☐ ☐ Camping or hiking.
2. ☐ ☐ ☐ ☐ Doing picture or crossword puzzles.
3. ☐ ☐ ☐ ☐ Playing party games (charades) or knowledge games (Trivial Pursuit™, Scrabble™).
4. ☐ ☐ ☐ ☐ Yard or landscape work.
5. ☐ ☐ ☐ ☐ Playing strategy games (like cards, chess, Go, Monopoly™).
6. ☐ ☐ ☐ ☐ Collecting old or new things (antiques, comics, coins, albums, autographs, etc.).
7. ☐ ☐ ☐ ☐ Playing computer, video or virtual reality games.
8. ☐ ☐ ☐ ☐ Playing sports, being on teams or part of a crew.
9. ☐ ☐ ☐ ☐ Going to museums, galleries, art shows, or cultural events.
10. ☐ ☐ ☐ ☐ Exercising vigorously.
11. ☐ ☐ ☐ ☐ Practicing self-defense.
12. ☐ ☐ ☐ ☐ Competing in individual sports such as running, swimming, or golf.
13. ☐ ☐ ☐ ☐ Vegetable or flower gardening.

14. ☐ ☐ ☐ ☐ Fixing up trails, doing park maintenance, and helping in beautification projects.

15. ☐ ☐ ☐ ☐ Farming or ranching.

16. ☐ ☐ ☐ ☐ Training, raising, or taking care of animals.

17. ☐ ☐ ☐ ☐ Sunbathing.

18. ☐ ☐ ☐ ☐ Watching people or phenomena (nature, birds, stars, tidepools, the sky).

19. ☐ ☐ ☐ ☐ Just sitting and daydreaming or meditating.

20. ☐ ☐ ☐ ☐ Watersports (swimming, surfing, skiing).

21. ☐ ☐ ☐ ☐ Building, making, or fixing things.

22. ☐ ☐ ☐ ☐ Reading books and magazines or going to the library.

23. ☐ ☐ ☐ ☐ Making jewelry, leather goods, or pottery, or working with wood or textiles.

24. ☐ ☐ ☐ ☐ Collecting photos, matchboxes, trinkets, or mementos.

25. ☐ ☐ ☐ ☐ Expressing myself artistically (painting, writing, music, sculpture).

26. ☐ ☐ ☐ ☐ Performing in skits, plays, dance, comedy, magic shows, fund-raisers, benefits, etc.

27. ☐ ☐ ☐ ☐ Going to parades, carnivals, or ethnic festivals.

28. ☐ ☐ ☐ ☐ Learning new things on my own or taking classes.

29. ☐ ☐ ☐ ☐ Teaching or training others.

30. ☐ ☐ ☐ ☐ Coaching sports.

31. ☐ ☐ ☐ ☐ Recreational travel or sightseeing.

32. ☐ ☐ ☐ ☐ Participating in spiritual or religious activities.

33. ☐ ☐ ☐ ☐   Belonging to a community service group, volunteering in an agency or program.

34. ☐ ☐ ☐ ☐   Helping neighbors or other people I know (informal volunteering).

35. ☐ ☐ ☐ ☐   Joining a club, social group, support group, or organization.

36. ☐ ☐ ☐ ☐   Working for a cause (political campaign, business, labor, ecology, etc.).

37. ☐ ☐ ☐ ☐   Air sports and activities (hot-air ballooning, skydiving).

38. ☐ ☐ ☐ ☐   Something I enjoyed as a child.

39. ☐ ☐ ☐ ☐   Something my grandparents did.

40. ☐ ☐ ☐ ☐   Something I always wanted to try.

Instructions for Using This Exercise:

Step 1: The general likes and dislikes (L/D) inventory
In the first column (Likes/Dislikes), put a plus (+) if you like an activity or think you would like to try it in the future. Put a minus (–) if you are certain this is something you really dislike. Be picky about your likes and dislikes; leave anything you have no strong opinion about blank.

Step 2: The group-preferences and stereotypes (G/S) inventory
Most of us prefer some types of people and not others. Which group of people would you most tend to avoid in your free time? People much older or younger than you? Single people? Couples or people with partners? Other types? Really think about it. Now, go back and, in the second column, G/S, put a check by each activity you associate with groups you avoid.

Step 3: The gender preferences (M/F) inventory
In the third column (M/F) mark those activities which you feel are done mostly by people of the opposite sex. So, if you are a male, put a mark by each activity which you feel is mostly done by females, and vice versa.

Step 4: Analysis
Go back and analyze the things you have given negative marks
in the first column (L/D). Do you see a pattern or correlation
between the ones you disliked and any of the items you have
marked under the G/S and M/F columns? What about between
the items you left blank in the first column and those marked in
the other two?

Step 5: The new options (O) inventory
Imagine how your life might change in the near future. Check off
the change which you have thought about most recently:

☐ losing a job   ☐ retiring

☐ having to move   ☐ children leave home

☐ divorce/separation   ☐ marriage

☐ death or loss of a mate   ☐ becoming physically

☐ other: or mentally limited

_____

_____

    Now, assume that the change you just checked off has taken
place. As a result, you may have to develop new strategies for
your leisure. Look over the next three statements and identify the
ones you find useful to do at this time. Then go back and thought-
fully fill in a key example.
    • You may have to modify or give up some of your favorite
leisure activities as a result of life changes. For example:

_____

    • Look back over the activities in the L/D column which you
have left blank or marked with a minus. Consider how your eval-
uations would change if your life changed dramatically. Mark
these new possibilities under the "O" column.
    Consider the value of approaching future leisure choices with

greater flexibility. In this regard, what advice might you conclude with?

_____

_____

_____

• I must always remind myself of the following:

The key thought is _____

_____

_____

_____

Successful Planning for Your Second Career

Your second career's success depends on the degree to which you think about or plan for it. Your planning must come from deep-seated values and passions. You must try to identify those leisure pursuits which stir your soul and your imagination.

Unfortunately, we don't have a college program or career center for people entering their second careers. If we did, you could probably earn a Senior Master's degree for planning your second career. You would be earning a degree for creating a "life-thesis." Appendix A has a sample of what such a program might look like.

Until such a learning-for-life program is founded, you'll have to find new passions and interests on your own. To help with this task, the next chapter concentrates on identifying your preferences, values, and interests. The process, which will be used throughout this book, is based on using the model most often used to help people weather a career change and locate new opportunities. I call my adapted model a "leisure search." To be successful in your search, you must give yourself permission to play. That's why this book is called *Serious Play.*

Don't put off until tomorrow the fun you can have today. Too often we promise to travel, take a class, or relax when we have more time or after we've retired. But we may never find that perfect future moment—it may never come.

Exercise 12:
Leisure Journal Assignment:
Reflection on My Second Career

Many different ideas have been discussed in this book. It is important to take a moment and reflect about the different notions running through your head and heart. In this activity, you will begin by writing about something on your mind and end by thinking about goals or dreams you wish to pursue.

Journal Starter: What's on My Mind . . .

1. Read over the starter questions below. Any of them may help you to sum up your thoughts about what you want to get out of life, now and in your future. Check off the set of questions that most seems to resonate within you.

☐ Think about age as it relates to your second career. At what age do you plan to start your second career life? Why is this a good age? How long would you like to live?

☐ Assuming your health and finances remain fairly stable, what would your ideal lifestyle be like? Write down a month's worth of typical activities. Describe yourself living to the fullest.

☐ We all need to have a Plan B in mind. Assuming that you have a goal, determine whether you have a Plan B. Begin by stating your goal for the next ten years. Then list possible problems you might encounter in the next phase of life (financial adjustment, family changes, career change or loss, health change, loss of spouse or partner, new marriage or partnership, change of location). Finally, brainstorm how you might change your plans or work around these problems. This list then becomes Plan B.

☐ It can be harmful to constantly compare the present to the past. Why? How does this retard the acceptance of change? How can you enjoy the past and still not compare it to the present?

☐ Think about goals and how they affect our lives. Then write about any goals that come to mind after reading the next set of questions.

- What goals did you have as a teenager or young adult?
- What goal are you considering for the next ten years ? What chance do you give yourself for fulfilling your goal (more or less than 50 percent)?
- How important to you is it to have a goal, strategy, or dream for your second career life?
- Which is more important: having a goal or reaching it? Why?
- How is a dream different from a goal?

☐ Make up your own topic.

2. Think about the topic you just checked off (or created). Then take one minute (time yourself) to make a list of ideas, questions, or feelings that you associate with this topic. Keep your pencil moving the whole time—if you can't think of a new word or phrase, just trace over the last thing you wrote. You want to avoid putting down the writing instrument and stopping the flow. By keeping the hand moving, you keep the mind active and this will help you tap hidden thoughts. List anything that comes into your mind.

3. Use this list as an initial brainstorm. Then express yourself on this topic in writing, drawing, or words and pictures. Use your previous list as a guide. Later, you may share anything you want from your writing, or simply listen to what others talk about.

Summing Up

Think about the different phases of your second career. At this point, which phase do you feel best describes you today?

- Phase 1: Graduating "Senior"
- Phase 2: The Action Years
- Phase 3: The Mellow Years
- Phase 4: Journey to the Interior
- Other: _____

 1. I think my most important task or challenge in this phase is:

_____

 2. One barrier I am facing right now is:

_____

 3. One small and simple change (or starter strategy) that I hope to implement in the near future is:

_____

 4. One year from now, I will feel very successful if I can say the following about my life:

_____

_____

 5. I plan to do the following to improve the quality of my leisure time:

_____

_____

_____

CHAPTER 5

Assessing Your Leisure Options

THIS CHAPTER IS chock-full of exercises and inventories that I have developed through my years of researching and presenting workshops on leisure wellness. That means that these activities are completely field-tested. Most people discover exciting new ideas in the process of trying them. Some of the comments made by past workshops in Washington state participants include:

If I were to reflect a year from now on changes in my leisure-use style or activity, I would expect to find my life enhanced and myself more interesting because of the changes brought about from the class ... a catalytic class.
—Training coordinator for a state agency
in Washington state

At age twenty-one I am new to the workforce in general, and working for the state in particular ... and there are lots of things to learn! I found this workshop very helpful in pointing out the benefits of balancing my work time with my leisure time.
—Office worker in an educational agency

Great stuff—timely. Mid-lifers and oldsters will find lots of goodies in Martin's workshop.
—Director of a retired seniors volunteer program

I found this workshop enlightening and entertaining. The information is useful; it made me think. I will use this information in my professional life as well as in my personal life.
                                        —Career counselor in a state college

I learned more about leisure in one day that I ever imagined. This would be great for retirees and counselors of all sorts.
                                        —Counselor at a chemical dependency
                                                    rehabilitation center

Take your time; don't try to complete all of the activities in one sitting. It works best if you finish items at a leisurely pace, giving yourself time to reflect in between. Find a place you enjoy reading and thinking. It might be a gazebo outdoors, a favorite cafe, your living room, or a cozy library. Relax with this book, and pencil in your answers to the various exercises.

Brainstorming and Imagining

In this chapter you'll visualize the possibilities available to you. You'll begin your examination of options by asking, "What if..." This brainstorming technique will flood your mind with memories of leisure activities you greatly enjoyed in the past. Other "what if..." questions will help you conjure up future possibilities. Following this creative random thinking, you'll use leisure-interest inventories to identify specific leisure options. The results of this assessment will be used in the next chapter to guide you in your community explorations. Thus, if you identify wood-carving as an interest through the exercises in this chapter, you'll use techniques in Chapter 6 to locate opportunities to join clubs or classes and learn from local experts. Once connected with community opportunities, you'll establish a momentum that will carry you down your leisure pathway for years to come.

Recalling the Past and Projecting into the Future

Some of your most enjoyable and powerful leisure experiences are locked away in childhood memories. Did you enjoy putting on a neighborhood magic show, finger-painting, or imagining fantastic images in the clouds? Did early camping experiences spark an interest in the environment? Did scouting or school service projects fill you with the desire to help others?

The following exercises will help you tap into memories of experiences that shaped your self-concept, and animated and guided your life. You'll recall leisure experiences from long ago, and will probably discover that some of your earliest hobbies, like magic or painting, still hold a special interest today.

Just as memories can help you revive long-lost passionate interests, projecting your leisure interests into the future can reveal buried or hidden aspirations. These are the leisure interests you keep putting off due to real and imagined barriers. When you think about things you *always* wanted to do, you give yourself permission to explore a whole new realm. What if you could magically travel to a future of new possibilities; what kind of science-fiction leisure would you enjoy?

Explore your past and future options in the following exercises. The ideas you glean from this process will become the seedbed for growing a new leisure ethic.

Exercise 13:
Treasure Chest Recollections and Future Projections

Recalling the Past

Early childhood experiences, hobbies, and leisure explorations are connected to some of our most passionate interests and basic talents. Recollecting early leisure experiences helps you brainstorm *renewable* possibilities. Often in later years or during retirement, people choose to revive long-lost leisure interests from days gone by.

1. What is the earliest leisure activity you remember doing with your family?

2. What is the earliest leisure activity you remember doing on your own?

_____

3. Have you ever helped others, volunteered, or served on committees where you had a really good time? What is one of your past favorite service or volunteer activities?

_____

4. Suppose the ghost of your childhood could come back to visit you today. Can you think of one thing you presently do or enjoy (your career, your present status, etc.) that would have shock you as your childhood "self?"

_____

5. What does this tell you about linking your past to your future?

_____

Projecting into the Future

What are your hopes and dreams for the future? Often, what you plan to do, whether you really think you'll follow through on it or not, is what you would *really* like to be doing with your time. Thus, this activity may help you to identify new interests.

6. To set the stage for future leisure, consider what toast you might make at a New Year's Eve party in 1999? Write your toast down.

_____

7. Look into the next century where there will be many new and exciting ways to spend your leisure. What is something you might enjoy doing that can't be done now. (Note: This is a science fiction leisure question. Use your imagination!)

---

8. End this future projection by returning to a more personal future: your own retirement. What is something you have always thought you would enjoy doing once you retire?

What Patterns Did You See?

Look over the information you have just assembled about your past and future, and then try to find some patterns. The following questions will help you identify a leisure motif or meaning amidst the brainstorm of information just recorded.

1. Were your interests associated with a particular season or day of the week?

2. Did you tend to share your leisure moments with certain people or did you do them alone?

3. Did the leisure activities from the past cost a lot of money?

4. As you look over the answers to the last exercise, did it occur to you that you had somehow neglected yourself or others?

5. Do you feel your leisure interests are well balanced or are they concentrated in a single area?

6. Did you uncover any forgotten or unfulfilled dreams worth investigating?

The Ultimate Dream

Have you ever bought a lottery ticket? What did you think about as you held that ticket to dreamland? In this next exercise you'll examine a leisure dream that changes. And throughout the change you'll become increasingly aware of your core leisure values.

Exercise 14:
Good News/Bad News Visualization

In this exercise, you will visualize how your life could change when good and bad news are combined. The changes you visualize may reveal something about the core values which influence your leisure choices.

Begin this exercise by coming up with six numbers that represent luck or happiness in your life. Write the numbers on the lottery ticket shown below.

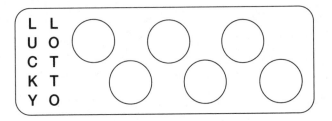

Good news! You've just won the lottery!

- After contemplating your lottery winnings, think about where you might go and whom you would take with you.

_____

- Suppose you decide to use the money to change your life. What is one thing you might do very differently in your work and leisure activities?

_____

- Oops! We goofed! You only have five of the six numbers and, therefore, only win $1000. Now where would you go and who would you take?

Bad news!

- It's getting worse . . . it turns out you didn't win after all. *Now* how will you spend your time? What would you choose to do on a free weekend for under $25?

Strange news

- In one day, you learn that you have won the lottery and that you also have a terminal illness. What might you plan to do with an increase in money and a decrease in time? What would you plan for a twenty-four-hour period? Who would you include in your plans?

Exercise 15:
Leisure Journal Assignment: Summing Up

Examine the different thoughts you had in these last two exercises. Pick two or more of the following questions to write about in your journal.

Questions and Reflections

1. Can you think of a childhood leisure experience you still enjoy today? Can you think of one leisure experience from your past that you'd like to revisit?

2. Some people say you can only enjoy leisure if you've got

lots of discretionary money. Why is this true or not true for you? What could you do with only $25?

3. Suppose you wanted to participate in an expensive sport like hot-air ballooning. Can you think of any inexpensive ways to begin getting involved? (Would reading magazines be sufficient for you? Would you be willing to trade services in a club in exchange for the opportunity to go up in someone's balloon?)

4. What does your toast to the new century tell you about yourself?

5. What is something you've thought of doing during retirement which ought to be investigated sooner rather than later.

6. A psychologist treating depressed people once observed that many of her clients found the greatest and most frequent satisfaction in the doing of simple, everyday, inexpensive activities. This included playing with the dog or cat, saying grace before a meal or counting one's blessings, and listening to music while laying on the couch. How do you feel about this idea? What do you think about the slogan, "quality leisure does not result from large quantities of money."

7. When you were contemplating living only twenty-four hours what did you come up with? Did you lean toward a wild idea or a simple (even conservative) plan?

Final Question

Which of your answers to the above questions best reflects some of your core values? Why?

Examining Preferences

After thinking across time and about your values, you're ready to focus on your leisure preferences. These preferences are like learning styles. There is no right or wrong, better or worse, preference.

It is simply a matter of deciding between two equally attractive options, and then choosing based on your preference, style, or feelings. In the afternoon on a crisp autumn day, will you choose to read indoors or tinker in the yard?

As with learning styles, one consciously—and often unconsciously—chooses or rejects a leisure activity based on personal preferences. For example, if you prefer being outdoors but live in a rainy climate, then you'll have to look for activities that are compatible with a long rainy season. It could be as simple as taking a winter class in a subject you hope to enjoy in the spring. Being aware of your need to be outdoors might also push you in the direction of exploring something as exotic as snow camping in the dead of winter. In other words, when you match your options to your temperament and personality, you'll be making stronger choices.

Your preferences generally reflect five kinds of choices:

- **Who** you enjoy spending leisure time with.
- **How you learn** best.
- **How you prefer to travel,** get around, or if you prefer not to travel.
- **Where** you are most comfortable in your free time.
- **When** you most enjoy doing things.

Let's take a moment to discuss these five types of preferences. Then, after considering each area, you will complete a preference inventory.

Who: General Observations about People Preferences

One of the most important leisure considerations is the "who" factor: who, if anyone, do you enjoy spending your free time with? As with any preference or style, your answer will depend somewhat on the specific activity and your evolving moods or interests. But, generally, you probably prefer to be with people or not. You either look upon your leisure time as an opportunity to meet or escape from people. Leisure experts have observed that people can generally be divided into three groups: those who like to spend the majority of their time alone, those who like to share a space during leisure time, but not necessary do the same thing (going to the mall with a friend but shopping separately, sitting in the living room together with one person reading and the other writing, going to the gym or a cafe together), and those who like to do the same activities as those they're with.

If you like being around others, try using your leisure encounters to strengthen or maintain bonds with partners or family members. Patsy B. Edwards, a pioneer in the leisure field, suggests that premarital counseling include a discussion about leisure interests and preferences. Similarly, we know that many couples today choose to cohabitate rather than jump into marriage. Prehabitation planning should probably include a mutual examination of leisure styles and preferences. Successful relationships build upon the need to recreate together—as well as separately. Likewise, if you take the time to discuss your changing leisure habits, your partners and family will support you (or join in), instead of watching from the sidelines with skepticism.

Which type of interaction do you prefer? Copy the list below, then check one:

I prefer spending most of my leisure time...

☐ Alone

☐ Around others (perhaps sharing the same space or same activity)

☐ With others (doing the same activity with another person)

Now give your blank copy to a special person you want to spend some time with. Each of you should complete this brief inventory separately and then compare answers. See if you have similar preferences. You may discover that this simple list speaks volumes.

Ultimately, you need to develop a strategy to accommodate and honor both your own preferences and the preferences of people you care about.

Accommodating others

1. Make two columns. In one, list things you and your partner enjoy doing apart; in the other, things you like to do together.

2. Next, try to find one "apart" thing you would be willing to do a little less of in order to spend more time with the other person.

3. Finally, try to identify one activity your partner enjoys, in which you could develop a greater interest, in the hope of learning more about (or getting closer to) them.

This activity will make you aware of the need to better balance your individual needs with your needs for companionship, to avoid harmful distortion.

One example of this type of distortion is workaholism, which infects relationships with the deadly virus of neglect. Consider the social costs incurred when partners or children feel neglected, costs that can include drug abuse, divorce, or anger directed at you.

The following journal entry shows how the author began a long examination of his own workaholism. Finding the balance is always a challenge. It begins with awareness of the problem:

I know that I can spend hours totally absorbed in writing or painting. I love it, I need to do it. But, both of these activities are solo enterprises. I find that when I have engaged in either for too long, that a certain pain invades my life. First, my lower back begins to ache. Then I look around, see my wife working outdoors in the garden and I feel a sense of aloneness.

In the past, she learned to stop trying to organize joint ventures because I ultimately would have a project that took me away. Now, I realize that if I want to avoid the pain, I must not only join her in the garden, but encourage her to plan events we both might enjoy. I have learned to welcome her vacation ideas and spontaneous plans—which interrupt my routine. Ever since I adopted this outlook, we've both been happier and my back and heart thank me.

Social interactions during leisure time play a special role in the lives of two groups of people. The quality of rehabilitation for drug abusers and the quality of life for retirees may both ultimately be linked to restructured lifestyles, new choices about what one chooses to do with free time and with whom one chooses to spend that time.

The choices made about the people one associates with during leisure are especially important during changes encountered during rehabilitation or retirement. According to drug and alcohol counselor Curt Rosler, successful rehabilitation begins the moment an addicted person tries to restructure his or her old lifestyle (see Appendix C for more details on leisure wellness and drug counseling). Breaking with old habits also means breaking with old friends and old ways of spending leisure time. By choosing new leisure activities, the client can begin to establish new contacts and new ways of spending time.

Rozanne Faulkner wrote a book detailing how therapeutic recreation helps heal drug dependency and other addictive patterns. She encourages addicted people to make an effort to choose free-time activities that promote positive family interactions. For example, if past holiday get-togethers resulted in bickering and excessive drinking, ask family members to get involved in suggesting new outlets, new options. Try staging the holiday events at a neutral home or restaurant, incorporating structured games, changing the beverage options, or modifying the length of visits.

Leisure choices made during retirement years can affect the quality of one's entire life. Retirees not only leave behind a job title, they also relinquish some of their most meaningful relationships. Many retirees report going through a period of social isolation, bewilderment, or withdrawal. To find and make new friendships, retired people must work all the harder to identify new leisure interests. The alternative is to try and sustain the old networks by remaining active in fund-raisers, alumni or retiree associations, and social events like the monthly poker game. Whichever path one follows, it is imperative that the retiree start exploring new networks or getting involved in workplace social events long before actual retirement.

How You Prefer to Learn

Once you begin to make more conscious choices about who you spend leisure with, it is helpful to examine how you want to learn during your free time. Most people think of schools and classes when they think about this, but some of your most powerful learning takes place in other settings. Moreover, the most exciting learning experience is the one you choose and design for yourself. People who direct their own learning experiences are called self-directed learners, and they come to realize that learning well leads to living well.

To illustrate this point, think of a talent you enjoy a great deal. Let's assume that this talent has even earned you a reputation or compliments. It may be a skill you use at work, or at home, in your church, neighborhood, or with an organization, club, or team. At times you have been called upon to share your talent or to teach others.

Consider how you acquired and honed this skill. You might have taken a class. But more than likely, you also received some special instruction from a master or mentor. In addition, you probably invested some of your own time, or perhaps money, researching and reading or attending workshops or classes in order to enhance your mastery. You were a self-directed learner.

Recalling how and where you gained this type of mastery will provide clues about your preferred learning style. Review the following story and try to identify Maria's learning preference or style.

At an early age, Maria's mother sent Maria to various painting classes. While she enjoyed working with the colorful oil paints, finger paints, and eventually acrylics, she never felt very secure in the summer art classes. Maria was never sure why one painting pleased people and another did not. In high school, she never even attempted to enroll in any art classes. Maria continued on her own, occasionally purchasing oil paints which she quietly used on vacation for fun.

Later in life, she entered a stressful period when painting offered her an escape. She could leave behind her troubles and enter a world of wild color, absorbed in the varying hues. One day, she showed her painting to a friend who was a high school painting teacher. The teacher's encouragement started Maria on a two-year painting escapade. She bought several books by artists she enjoyed, cut out pictures from magazines, and collected sample postcards by artists she saw in galleries.

After the first year, she brought several samples of her work to a gallery owner. The owner criticized her draftsmanship. This stopped Maria cold in her palette. After a few months, she decided to try and improve her drawing skills, but she knew she didn't want to take a class for all the old reasons.

Maria went back to the art teacher and traded a phone answering machine for five personal drawing lessons. The drawings improved, confidence returned, and she filled many canvases with brightly colored images. By the end of the second year she was invited to show her works in an urban gallery. Maria had stayed true to her learning style, and as a result remained highly motivated.

If you were asked to label Maria's learning preference or style, how would you describe it?

☐ Taking classes from experts

☐ Reading books

☐ Joining a group of people

☐ Learning on one's own (without the help of others)

☐ Watching others, or with assistance from others when one gets stuck

There is no precise label for Maria's learning style because she combines aspects of different learning options, as do most of us. While Maria prefers to learn on her own, she also enjoys seeking out mentors who enrich her self-directed learning adventures. Being aware of your own learning style(s) or preferences is critical to lifelong learning success. And the ability to learn is the key to mastering new leisure arenas.

Learning During Your Second Career

Retirees often feel hampered by the stereotype of senior citizens with diminished mental capacity. Imprisoned by this prejudice, some seniors retreat from learning, especially in formal school settings. Your first lesson is to break this unholy mold!

Most gerontology and retirement experts point out that mental capacity does not diminish with age. While older people may tend to learn more slowly, the *capacity* to learn is not diminished. Indeed, it is enhanced by a reservoir of life experience. Some of our greatest artists and scientists did their best work late in life.

One's second career (the retirement years) may be the perfect time to learn about previously neglected subjects. You might begin exploring computers, finances, repairs, and remodeling. Or it might be the right time to investigate creative talents: arts, music, photography, and writing. This is also a time when individuals often develop an interest in history, local governments, and community or civics groups.

These same principles apply to older people living in full-care nursing homes. In *Enhance Your Destiny, Dare to Build a Second Life,* Elwood Chapman wrote about two groups of nursing-home residents who were given regular care. One group was given additional responsibilities (tending plants, deciding on meals and movies, planning entertainment programs). A Dr. Langer, who conducted the study, found that the more active and involved group demonstrated greater alertness, confidence, and less depression. They showed fewer symptoms of disabilities associated with advanced aging.

Langer concluded that mindlessness greatly contributes to aging. Lifelong learning is a powerful aging retardant! To benefit from this youthful elixir, try to identify your learning preferences and use them to exercise your mental talents.

How You Prefer to Travel

Are you willing to travel great distances to windsurf? How much time are you willing to spend on the bus or freeway in the pursuit of a leisure interest? Can you travel at night, do you have safety concerns?

Or do you prefer staying around home in your spare time? In one study, the overwhelming majority of people reported that they enjoyed spending the majority of their free time at home.

While transportation may not appear to be a complicated subject, it is perhaps one of the most common barriers to achieving leisure wellness. Transportation logistics are particularly challenging for disabled, poor, young, and elderly people. The great irony is that these various groups of people may be in the greatest need of healthy leisure experiences, but are denied access due to transportation limits.

There are no magical solutions to the transportation dilemma, but several strategies *can* minimize a lack of transportation. Many mass transit systems now provide personalized and individualized services, car pooling options, ride sharing, and even rentals.

Assertiveness is vital. You need to sit down with significant people in your life, the ones who possess a means of transport, and communicate the importance of getting transportation assistance to leisure outlets. Finally, consider barter. Could you exchange services for rides? Wash a car, baby-sit, cook, or house-sit in exchange for rides or the keys.

Where You Are Most Comfortable

The places you prefer to spend your leisure time often depend on the type of activity you choose. But, if you stop to reflect for a moment, you'll probably find that you spend the majority of your leisure time in certain types of places. The menu that one typically chooses from includes the following:

- Urban
- Rural
- Indoor
- Outdoor
- At Home
- Away from Home
- Foreign

When: Time Preferences

As we've already noted, time is a perplexing subject, particularly as affluent members of Western civilization increasingly feel that they have more money and less leisure time. Many feel that their pace or schedule is becoming compressed and their free time fragmented. In addition, many of us fail to examine how we use or abuse our time.

Examining your time *preferences* is a much simpler matter. What is your favorite day of week or season of the year? Are you morning person? Do you love the autumn? What do you feel is the best time for you to start a new venture?

Assessing Your Leisure Preferences

Having discussed the various aspects of leisure preferences, you are now ready to complete the Leisure Preference Inventory. Find a nice place to relax and see what happens. Later, you will try to match your preferences to specific leisure options or interests.

Exercise 16:
Leisure Style and Preference Inventory

In this exercise, you'll review preferences from eight different categories. Then, you'll try to identify or prioritize your top preferences.

Begin by reading the choices in each of the eight categories. More than one preference may appeal to you in each category. You need not check off every choice presented in this survey. Try to choose and concentrate on the ones that matter the *most* to you. Limiting yourself in this way will make it easier to hone in on your top choices towards the end of the exercise. You may want to mark items lightly at first and then go back and darken the items that appeal to you the most.

1. Places

I prefer spending my free time:

☐ indoors   ☐ outdoors   ☐ both indoors and outdoors

☐ near home   ☐ away from home   ☐ at home

☐ in the city   ☐ in the country   ☐ both city and country

☐ other: _____

2. Transportation

I prefer to spend my leisure:

☐ near my home because I dislike traveling or it's hard to get around.

☐ anywhere, because I don't mind traveling to get involved in a leisure activity.

I prefer to travel by:

☐ bus   ☐ car   ☐ carpool   ☐ bike

☐ other: _____

Other transportation issues (example: I will need to trade chores like washing cars to barter for rides or borrow a car) and preferences:

_____

_____

3. People

I prefer to do things with:

☐ close friends   ☐ people I know   ☐ people I don't know

I like to do things:

☐ alone   ☐ *with* others   ☐ *around* others (near others but not with them)

I prefer people who are:

☐ like me (e.g. same age, gender, or background)   ☐ different from me

4. Level of involvement

I prefer:

☐ doing things or participating   ☐ watching others

5. Skills

I would enjoy leisure time where I'd use these kinds of skills:

☐ working physically, with hands, body, or machines.

☐ reading or mental skills (writing, reading, studying, thinking).

☐ working with numbers in some way.

☐ helping, teaching, or working with people in other ways.

☐ working with animals or plants.

☐ doing crafts, music, or other artistic or expressive activities.

☐ exploring the spiritual areas of life.

☐ working with skills that are the same as the ones I use(d) at work.

☐ working with skills that are different from the ones I use at work.

☐ other skills:

_____

6. Times

I prefer having my leisure experiences:

☐ on weekends   ☐ on weekdays   ☐ it doesn't matter

☐ mornings   ☐ afternoons   ☐ evenings

☐ planned   ☐ unplanned   ☐ it doesn't matter

☐ during seasons or holidays such as:

_____

_____

7. Money resources

How much money can you afford to spend on major leisure interests each week, or per occasion?

☐ $0-10   ☐ $11-50   ☐ over $50

Assume that a new leisure interest costs more than you could afford. Maybe you'd have to pay a membership fee, or buy tools. What would you be willing to do to get involved?

☐ Wait until I saved enough money.

☐ Offer to do volunteer work at an organization in exchange for membership or services.

☐ Trade services or things for lessons, memberships, or equipment usage.

☐ Start at a low-cost level by learning on my own, visiting clubs, reading magazines, or using tapes.

8. Learning methods

Exploring leisure means learning. Remember, the Greek word for

leisure was "schole" which became our root word for "school."
You can learn in many different ways, including attending a class,
watching others, studying on your own, joining a group, and finding a mentor to assist you. This inventory will help you review
your preferred learning styles and may suggest ways to pursue a
new leisure activity.

One of my favorite classes in the past was:

_____

I enjoyed it because:

_____

I have taught myself how to:_____

I did this by:

☐ reading about it   ☐ asking people   ☐ watching others

☐ other: _____

I have enjoyed learning things in:

☐ camps   ☐ seminars   ☐ workshops

☐ classes   ☐ conferences

I prefer to learn by:

☐ taking classes from experts.

☐ reading books.

☐ joining a group of people.

☐ learning on my own (without help from others).

☐ watching others, or with assistance from others when I get
  stuck.

☐ my own special way, which is:

_____

Prioritizing Your Preferences

Go back and think about all the preferences you marked off in the previous eight preference categories. Then try to identify the most important preferences relating to people, places, times, and two other preferences of your choice. List or describe them in the boxes below. You'll reuse this information later.

People	Places	Times		

In Chapter 2, Exercise 7 (the Environmental Scan), you took an initial look at your preferences. You may wish to review your work in Chapter 2 before continuing. Look for clues that might point to your most important preferences. See if these clues corroborate choices you made in this exercise. Then complete the chart below.

People	Places	Times		
corroborating clues	corroborating clues	corroborating clues	corroborating clues	corroborating clues

What Can I Do? What Are My Options?

When I was a little boy caught in the never-ending dog days of August, I'd wander up to my mother in the kitchen and whine, "What can I do?" She'd always respond with, "Spit in a shoe. Now go out and play." Sometimes as an adult, I still find myself on a lazy Sunday morning, wondering about what I would like to do. This last inventory is designed to help you answer that question.

It's time to take on a list of specific leisure activities. The following inventory is modeled after a job interest inventory. In a job interest test, you might see managerial and clerical job titles listed under business clusters, social worker and teacher under service occupations clusters, and so on. In *this* exercise, all similar leisure activities are clustered together, forming eight major groups.

This survey is meant to stimulate you in two ways. First, it will help you review the things you have enjoyed doing in the past or enjoy right now. Second, it will remind you about those things you'd like to do in the future but have put off or forgotten.

As you review each item on the list, use check marks to indicate the strength of your interest in a given activity. Put one check mark if the activity is something you've thought about doing but have never actually tried. Put two check marks if you have actually tried the activity and would like to do it again in the future. If the activity is something you're doing now and wish to continue with, then it is probably a fairly strong leisure interest and it deserves three check marks.

After you finish, you'll be able to identify your strongest cluster areas by totaling the number of marks. Thus, if you find that a current interest in being a scout leader is not feasible, you can look for another similar activity, such as being a Big Brother/Big Sister volunteer, within the same service cluster area.

Most people know some of their specific strengths and interests. They are aware that they enjoy collecting antiques, going camping, and visiting coffeeshops. However, when you stand back and look at the visual display of check marks in given clusters, you might gain a new perspective on your leisure interests. Don't be surprised if you find that one cluster has fewer total checks than another, and similarly one area you'd completely forgotten about now triggers thoughts of many new choices.

This survey is a product of several years of research and accumulation of ideas. While it cannot cover everything, it *is* one of the most comprehensive surveys available. The community service section alone is unique in leisure interest surveys. Take your time completing it in order to get the most out of it.

Exercise 17:
Kimeldorf's Leisure Options Inventory

Use this inventory to identify old leisure interests you wish to renew, or pinpoint new ones to explore. After you read each leisure option, rate each item with check marks or leave it blank. Be picky, choose things that would be practical for you to do in the future (but define "practical" in your own terms). Use a pencil so you have the option of changing your responses.

✓ Single check by new item you have not yet done, but would really like to try in the future.

✓✓ Double check by any thing you have done in the past and would like to renew in the future.

✓✓✓ Triple check by anything you currently enjoy doing and wish to continue.

Please accept the fact that in any comprehensive inventory there will always arise the need to use one item more than once. For instance, the activity of skydiving could be used in the subgroups related to "air sports" or "high-risk activities" as well as "outdoors." Repeating the activity on more than one list, increases the chance that you will have sufficiently diverse examples to help stimulate your thinking about the many possibilities.

Sports, Fitness, and Other High Energy Activities

One Person or Small Group Activities

1. Aerobics, gymnastics, jumprope
2. Air sports (gliding, skydiving)
3. Archery
4. Marksmanship, shooting

5. Boating, sailing

6. Cycling

7. Weight training

8. Golf

9. Horseback riding

10. Ice sports (skiing, sledding, skating, sailing)

11. Jogging, running, speed-walking

12. Karate, self-defense, boxing, wrestling

13. Fencing

14. Driving off-road vehicles

15. Racing (cars, bikes, trucks, etc.)

16. Roller skating, skateboarding

17. Tennis, badminton

18. Handball, racquetball, squash

19. Watersports (swimming, diving, surfing, water-skiing, windsurfing)

20. High-risk activities: bungie jumping, parachuting

Team Sports

21. Baseball/softball

22. Basketball

23. Bowling

24. Football

25. Soccer, rugby

26. Track and field

27. Volleyball

28. Hockey (field, ice)

Other high-energy ideas:

_____

Games (Active or Inactive) and Friendly Competitions

Mental and Simulation Games

1. Card games
2. Computer (electronic) games, artificial intelligence, interactive games, virtual reality, simulations
3. Games of chance (bingo, dice, roulette)
4. Knowledge games (Trivial Pursuit™)
5. Puzzles (pictures, words, numbers)
6. Puzzles you handle (Rubik's Cube™, string games)
7. Real-life-based games (Monopoly™, Payday™)
8. Strategy games (checkers, chess, dominoes)
9. Word games (crossword puzzles, Scrabble™)
10. Entering contests

Active Games (also see nature and outdoor)

11. Arcade, video games requiring manual dexterity
12. Treasure and scavenger hunts
13. Billiards, pool
14. Charades, other party games
15. Croquet
16. Marbles, jacks
17. Darts, other target games
18. Frisbee™, Hula Hoop™, hopscotch
19. Horseshoes
20. Miniature golf
21. Shuffleboard
22. Curling
23. Jumprope
24. Organizing parties

25. Ping pong
26. Yo-yos
27. War games
28. "New games" (noncompetitive games based on challenge and/or cooperation)

Other ideas:

_____

Nature and Outdoor

Nature

1. Astronomy, stargazing
2. Beachcombing
3. Bird-watching
4. Camping
5. Canoeing, rafting, boating
6. Nature walks
7. Hiking, backpacking
8. Mountain climbing
9. Outdoor cooking, picnics
10. Protecting the environment
11. Rock hunting
12. Sunbathing
13. Tide pool hunting
14. Watching scenery and wildlife
15. Weather- or sky-watching
16. Orienteering, exploring, spelunking
17. High risk activities (wilderness survival)

Animals or Plants

    18. Breeding, training, raising, caring for animals

    19. Flowers (arranging, horticulture)

    20. Fresh or saltwater fishing

    21. Rodeo, bullfighting

    22. Hunting and/or trapping animals

    23. Plant identification, hunting wild edibles

    24. Clamming

    25. Farming or ranching

    26. Training, exhibiting, showing animals or plants

    27. Gardening, growing vegetables

    28. Landscaping

Other outdoor ideas:

Crafts and Hobbies

    1. Amateur radio, Morse code, cryptography

    2. Bookbinding and design

    3. Calligraphy or handwriting analysis

    4. Candle- or soap-making

    5. Cooking, baking, cake decorating, gourmet clubs

    6. Electronics, stereo, kits, etc.

    7. Flower arranging, topiary, dry flower displays

    8. Folk art or crafts (whittling, stoneware, found objects, totems, etc.)

    9. Interior decorating

    10. Tool and instrument making

    11. Toy making or kite making and flying

12. Leather and textiles
13. Making things from kits
14. Masonry or rockery
15. Metalwork, jewelry, welding, casting, blacksmithing
16. Model building, miniatures (railroads, cars, dolls, etc.)
17. Paper crafts, origami
18. Pottery, ceramics
19. Programming, computer designing or simulations, problem solving activities, playing with robotics or artificial intelligence
20. Repair or maintenance (cars, appliances)
21. Sewing and needlecrafts (knitting, crocheting)
22. Unusual crafts: tattooing, taxidermy
23. Upholstery
24. Weaving, macramé, quilting, basketry
25. Wine or beer making
26. Woodworking, carpentry, furniture restoration
27. Working with plastics or resins
28. Bookkeeping, playing stocks, budgeting and planning

Other ideas:

_____

Collecting Things

1. Antiques, primitive artifacts
2. Art pieces, jewelry
3. Autographs
4. Books, manuscripts, letters
5. Bumper stickers, buttons, pins with slogans
6. China, glassware, demitasse sets

7. Clocks, watches, other timepieces

8. Coins, stamps, trading cards, or other recognized rare collectibles

9. Dolls

10. Hats

11. License plates

12. Low-cost collections or things from trips (bottle caps, keys, insulators, bottles, matches, decals, cans)

13. Magazines

14. Masks

15. Models, miniatures

16. Music, sheet music

17. Myth, folklore

18. Natural objects (rocks, shells, flowers, butterflies, insects, etc.)

19. Personal memorabilia (mementos, souvenirs, buttons, matches)

20. Photos, postcards, travel mementos

21. Political campaign items

22. Records

23. Religious objects

24. Stuffed animals

25. Swapables (items from garage sales, swap meets, flea markets)

26. Tapestries

27. Objects representing friendship, peace, and cooperation

28. Weapons, military objects, medals

Other collectibles:

_____

Arts, Music, Performing, and Self-Expression Activities

1. Juggling, clowning, circus performing
2. Costume design
3. Customizing cars
4. Dancing (ballet, folk, belly, ballroom, etc.)
5. Designing clothes
6. Dramatic activities
7. Drawing, illustrating, cartooning
8. Holiday performer (Santa Claus, Easter Bunny)
9. Glass making or stained glass
10. Interior design, decorating
11. Lettering, calligraphy
12. Marching, drill team, cheerleading, being in parades
13. Mask making, stage makeup
14. Modeling, beauty competitions
15. Music making (vocal, instrument, sing-alongs, whistling, etc.)
16. Painting
17. Performing magic
18. Personal writing (letters, diaries/journals, memoirs, scrapbooks, autobiography)
19. Photography or darkroom
20. Printing, lithography, etching
21. Public speaking, storytelling
22. Performing plays or comedy, stage pageants, shows, entertainment
23. Puppetry, ventriloquism
24. Sculpturing (wood, stone, sand, ice)

25. Writing poetry, greeting cards, lyrics, music

26. Writing nonfiction, fiction, drama

27. Producing media products (film, video, radio)

Other creative ideas:

Entertaining, Socializing, and Relaxing

Attending, Observing, or Participating in:

1. Amusement parks, carnivals, or a circus

2. Bookstores, libraries, or learning centers

3. Courtroom, public hearings, or legislative sessions

4. Community events (celebrations, displays)

5. Food and entertainment (dining out, night club)

6. Special people events involving celebrities or experts

7. Media events (TV, film, video, radio, records, tapes)

8. Parades, pageants, or rodeos

9. Performances with entertainment emphasis (benefits, comedy, folk music, or music festivals)

10. Stores, galleries, resorts (browsing or shopping)

11. Nature (watching the sky, stars, clouds, flora, fauna)

12. Sports events

13. Trade shows, demonstrations

Primarily Socializing

14. Dating, singles group activities, social events

15. Joining a club or group with a special purpose (community service, support group, collectors, games, jazz, seniors, computer bulletin board)

16. Meeting others for coffee, drinks, or food; meeting at galleries or cultural events, hiking or walking together

17. Entertaining, planning, or attending parties
18. Visiting and/or reminiscing with family or friends in person or by telephone

Relaxation

19. Daydreaming, meditating
20. Doing nothing, relaxing
21. Enjoying massage, sauna, spa, acupuncture
22. Puttering around the home, doing chores
23. Reading books
24. Practicing yoga, tai chi

Traveling and Exploring

25. Taking a navigation or challenge course
26. Driving special vehicles (recreational or off-road vehicles, underwater travel, hot air balloons)
27. Touring, sight-seeing, vacationing by myself, or with others (car, bus, train, boat)
28. Taking long trips, traveling abroad (foreign countries)

Other ideas:

_____

Education, Self-Improvement, Cultural or Spiritual

Education and Self-Improvement

1. Art history
2. Astronomy
3. Biofeedback
4. Criminology and law
5. Environment
6. Foreign language or culture

7. Health, wellness, medicine

8. Investing and financial planning

9. Leadership development

10. Natural science

11. Philosophy

12. Repair and restoration techniques

13. Retirement planning

14. Self-improvement (diets, self-esteem, family relations, parenting)

15. Self-awareness (careers, leisure, relationships, etc.)

16. Teaching others

Cultural, Learning about or Attending:

17. Ethnic and neighborhood festivals

18. Performances (concert, dance, storytelling, theater)

19. Family traditions, genealogy

20. Museums, galleries, exhibits

Spiritual and Philosophical

21. Going to church, synagogue, mosque, temple, or other religious place; attending religious retreats

22. Praying, meditating, or studying spiritual ideas on your own

23. Studying philosophy, mysticism, metaphysics, psychic phenomena, or developing my own philosophy

Learning and Teaching Styles I Enjoy Most

24. Doing a personal assessment or inventory, setting goals

25. Attending lecture series, classes, workshops

26. Learning from a coach or mentor, in an apprenticeship-style situation

27. Engaging in self-directed independent study

28. Watching television, media productions, public access TV, using a computer

Other ideas:

_____

Community Service

Cultural and Arts

1. Beautification project
2. Contributing artistic skills to community display of artwork, contributing art to fund-raisers
3. Assisting in a museum or library, as a guide or docent
4. Organizing cultural events, shows, etc.
5. Teaching others how to paint, sing, dance, etc.

Education, Mentors, Youth

6. Teaching or training others
7. Being a Big Brother or Big Sister
8. Speaking or volunteering in school or church
9. Being a scout leader
10. Being a tutor or teacher's aide

Environmental, Outdoor, and Recreational

11. Camp aide
12. Parks volunteer
13. Special Olympics aide

Health and Emergency

12. Crisis clinic
13. Hospital, hospice, convalescent center, or residential care facility volunteer

14. Red Cross

15. Search and rescue

16. Volunteer fire department

Intergenerational

17. Latchkey programs

18. Meals on Wheels

19. Buddy, partner, or pals-type programs

20. Senior center

Nonprofit and Public Organizations

21. Going to school board or town council meetings

22. Going to hearings or giving testimony

23. Religious group or club

24. Senior groups (AARP, Meals on Wheels, RSVP, SCORE, Emeritus)

25. Salvation Army

26. Service groups (Kiwanis, Lions, Rotary)

27. Traveler's Aid

28. United Way

29. Volunteering in an institution or agency (corrections, welfare, employment, mental health)

30. Volunteering on an advisory board

Neighborhood

31. Assisting neighborhood group

32. Crime watch or prevention

33. Escort, safety service

34. Food co-op worker

35. Welcome wagon

Political and Advocacy

36. American Legion or Veterans

37. Environment (Greenpeace, Sierra Club, etc.)

38. League of Woman Voters

39. People First, Association of Retarded Citizens, organization for the handicapped

40. Political activism in parties or general causes (demonstrations, petitions, organizing, speaking, attending conventions, sitting on advisory boards)

41. Single-issue involvement (voting, peace, unemployment, drinking and driving)

42. Urban League, women's groups, immigrants' groups, or any group formed around a cultural similarity

43. Working for candidates

Poverty, Assistance, and Collecting Needed Items

44. Collecting food at work or door-to-door

45. Food bank volunteering

46. Helping organize a way to collect money

47. Homeless shelter

48. Raising money for cultural events

49. Walk-a-thons, Dance-a-thons

50. Women's shelter

Supporting a Group (fund-raising, budget, chair, etc.)

51. Business group (chamber of commerce, Junior Achievement, small business)

52. Professional group (educators' association, engineers, nurses, etc.)

53. Special interest group (computer users, car racers, garden club, woodcarvers, weavers)

Other ideas:

_____

Picking Three New Pathways

Look for a pattern. What group contains most of your interests? The following questions will help you examine the larger categories of leisure clusters, and then narrow them down to three individual leisure options.

Examining Leisure Clusters

Write the total check marks you had for each cluster area:

___ A. Sports, Fitness, and High Energy

___ B. Game and Friendly Competitions

___ C. Nature and Outdoor

___ D. Crafts and Hobbies

___ E. Collecting Things

___ F. Arts, Music, Performing, and Self-Expression

___ G. Entertaining, Socializing, and Relaxing

___ H. Education, Self-Improvement, Cultural, Spiritual

___ I. Community Service (enter only half the total marks)

Now match the cluster-letters (A through I) to the questions below. If you have a hard time answering any question, use the number of checks beneath each cluster as a guide. However, you need not base your answer solely on the number of check marks.

1. Which two clusters above gave you the most choices? __ __

2. Which one has the least to offer you?   ___

3. Which cluster is one you'd like to explore the most?   ___

4. Which one is most like your past or present job?   ___

5. Which one is most unlike your past or present job?   ___

Choosing Three Individual Leisure Options

Now, for the next part of your leisure search, focus in on trying to choose three options to explore. If you pick options that are unusual or new to you, it will make the rest of the leisure search more interesting. Choose activities you have always wondered about, or ones that are absolutely brand new—unless you find that leisure interests from the past really fire up your imagination. Consider your preferences as you choose the three.

If you can't easily decide on your top three, or you want to examine your options further, then complete the Decision Making Grid, below.

Three leisure options I'd like to explore next in my leisure search are:

1. _____

2. _____

3. _____

Exercise 18:
Decision-Making Grid (Optional)

If you find it difficult to make a final choice, use the following "grid" process. This technique compares your top leisure preferences with six leisure activities that interest you. Then you'll compare each activity against your preferences and the result will be a prioritized list of leisure options. A sample of the grid is shown next.

In the sample chart, Sheila found that items 1, 5, and 6 (golf, railroads, and sky-diving) contained the most number of matches with her preferences (be with others, be outdoors, evening time, do most of the time, involve physical activity). Each item has at least three or more matches (or "X's") while the activities for items 2, 3, and 4 only matched her preferences in two or fewer instances. This helped Sheila prioritize her top six leisure options and then select her top three from that list.

Sheila's Grid: My Top Five Preferences					
Six Possible Interests	People *Be with others*	Places *Be outdoors*	Times *Evenings*	Other *Do all the time*	Other *Be physical*
1. A previous interest *Golf*	X	X	X		X
5. New Option *Model railroading*	?		X	X	X
6. New Option *Sky diving*	X	X	?		X

Use this grid to help you identify and prioritize the three leisure options you would like to investigate next.

1. Transfer your leisure preferences from Exercise 16 (Leisure Style And Preference Inventory) to the top row of the grid (the row labeled *My Top Five Preferences*)

2. Find the first left-hand column, *Six Possible Interests*. In this column, going down, list three interests from the past (renewable) and three new interests.

3. Then cross check your interests against your preferences. As in Sheila's example, your goal is to see which leisure activities contain the greatest match with your preferences.

	My Top Five Preferences				
Six Possible Interests	People	Places	Times	Other	Other
1. A past activity I might renew					
2. A past activity					
3. A past activity					
4. A new area to explore					
5. A new area to explore					
6. A new area to explore					

The completed grid will help you select the three leisure options that have the greatest potential for you, those that would be the most fun to investigate. Rank your top three choices, assuming that you'll start working on the first one and use the other two as fallback alternatives, if necessary.

Analyzing Your Leisure Portfolio

What did these exercises show you? Did you find your interests concentrated in one or two clusters, or did they seem to be spread out across several? Did you perhaps question why I wanted you to do this in the first place?

The approach used in this book is based on proven career exploration methods. Job seekers are advised to have more than one occupational target in a tight labor market. It's simply a matter of developing a Plan B and even a Plan C.

Backup plans are equally important to the leisure search process discussed in the next chapter. Contingency planning serves as insurance in your search for leisure wellness. It is similar to balancing a financial portfolio. You simply don't want to put all of your eggs in one leisure basket.

Seeking Balanced Leisure

Concentrating on only one leisure interest can lead to a leisure mania. An addicted runner grows to accept shin splints as normal, other dysfunctional types shut out the world by pasting their noses into a book during every spare moment. Couch kings and queens inject every spare moment with the cathode rays emanating from a television. These humorous (or tragic) images of a leisure addiction can have unhealthy side effects.

A workaholic does one thing well—to excess—work. Leisure-aholics are the same. To avoid a preoccupation or addiction with a single job or single leisure activity, you need to create balance. Balance must be achieved not only between work and leisure, but also within leisure itself. The pursuit of variety is the key to balanced leisure.

Special attention to leisure addiction must be paid by those undergoing drug treatment or rehabilitation, and those who have retired, and are now entering their second career. Even if you are not a member of these two groups, consider the lessons which might also apply to your own situation.

Leisure Addiction and Drug Addiction

In her book *Therapeutic Recreation in Drug Treatment Settings,* Rozanne Faulkner claims that substance abusers often substitute a leisure addiction for drug addiction. Counselors and concerned people are advised to watch for clients who project their malady onto their leisure choices. She cites examples of clients formerly addicted to depressants who went on to choose passive, reflective, or meditative activities. On the other hand, she observed individuals trying to escape from stimulants who engage only in active, competitive sports or games. The manic focus on a single activity creates a kind of leisure that no longer refreshes. The mania or addiction hastens burnout, which leads to other problems.

Flexibility during Retirement

Flexibility is also a key to success in the second careers. Successful transition to retirement often depends on creative substitution of old activities with new ones. You will want to know when it is time to turn eighteen holes of golf into nine, or when bus tours should replace RV adventures. Flexibility helps one gracefully adapt to the aging process.

In Chapter 4, you will find a special exercise geared to helping retirees and senior citizens develop flexible attitudes. If you feel your leisure decision-making lacks flexibility, try that exercise now, regardless of your age. Exercise 19, Balanced Leisure, will help you develop a balanced leisure portfolio.

Exercise 19:
Balanced Leisure

Use this inventory to identify the kinds of leisure experiences that will bring you balance and a sense of being well-rounded. You need not try to find an idea for each of the fifteen items. (You don't want to become addicted to balance), but *do* try for at least eight or more.

1. An activity I'd like to renew from my younger days is:

_____

2. An energizing, stimulating, exhilarating activity is:

_____

3. A relaxing, calming, quiet thing to do would be:

_____

4. An activity that uses my vocational skills is:

_____

5. An activity that doesn't use my vocational skills is:

_____

6. Spiritual, religious, or otherworldly experiences that interest me are:

_____

7. Creative activities (artistic, design, problem solving) are:

_____

8. Educational or self-improvement projects are:

_____

_____

9. Things I enjoy doing at home are:

_____

_____

10. Ways to enjoy a change in my scenery are:

_____

_____

11. Transportable or quick things I could do (on break, while commuting, in spare moments) are:

_____

_____

12. Something to do with my partner or best friends is:

_____

13. Some things to do with my family are:

_____

_____

14. Some things I enjoy doing alone are:

_____

_____

15. Something brand-new to me is:

_____

Go back over these the ideas you listed in this exercise and circle the five that are most appealing to you. Try to pick things that give you the greatest variety. Then develop a plan for sampling as many of these as you can. What kind of schedule or approach might offer you the greatest variety and balance in your leisure?

CHAPTER 6

The Leisure Search

HE STORY OF humankind quietly unfolds where the jungle submits to the wide-open plains. A small band of hunters and gatherers intrudes upon the scene. Each day the hunters meet to plan their daily search for survival. Several millennia later, a huge number of urban dwellers are living in an information jungle. The inhabitants have traded in their bows and spears for keyboards and handshakes. Instead of hunting for dinner, today's tribe searches for career and leisure opportunities.

In the past, you could hunt for what you needed with your band of comrades. But in today's modern, atomized existence we often go it alone. Research shows that hunting alone, particularly for work, is a task fraught with discouragement, which reduces effort and effectiveness.

In the late 1970s and early 1980s, several groups demonstrated that job hunters could become more effective, handle more rejection, and persevere longer if they hunted in our modern tribal form: the self-help support group. These self-directed groups were known as job clubs, and they helped unemployed people fine-tune their job-search skills and sustain the hunt in the face of persistent challenges.

Now, imagine what it would be like to join a leisure-search club. In such a setting, the search for leisure might become a recreational activity in itself, echoing the values of earlier cultures such as Greece and Crete, in which people equated well-developed leisure pursuits with personal improvement. Unfortunately, few of us have the opportunity to join such a leisure-search class or group (at this time, most of us cannot), but you can still get some of the benefits by conducting your leisure search with friends or a partner.

The Essential Task Begins

This chapter provides the tools you'll need to begin building a new chapter in your own leisure life. You'll start by becoming a leisure information hunter and gatherer, searching for clues and tracking down leisure opportunities in your community. Thus, if you're interested in wood carving, you'll learn how to gather information about wood carving classes, clubs, supplies, and literature. The hunt culminates when you come face-to-face with your quarry: an expert wood carver. This person will have the potential to offer advice or serve as role model or mentor.

The leisure search concept is patterned after job-search models in which the job-seeker gathers leads about openings using networking, library references, and in-person interviews. Richard Bolles, author and career expert, points out in *What Color Is Your Parachute* that the job search is basically a search for information. The leisure search we are about to embark on incorporates the same effective information-searching techniques.

Unlike a job search, this search for leisure opportunities is not competitive. However, it can also be more difficult to structure at first because it is not supported by the traditional information sources found in a job search: want ads, career centers, expert advice in books and seminars, etc. Since you cannot look up "wood carver" in the classified section of a newspaper, you must do a bit of networking to find the people and information you need. This chapter contains detailed information on how to apply successful networking techniques to your search for new leisure options.

Step 1: Gathering General Information

Before finding your expert, you'll need to gather some general information. Suppose you wanted to investigate hot-air ballooning.

You must get answers to the following general questions:

- Who does it?
- When do people meet?
- Where is it done?
- How can I get started?

In job finding, the people who give you this kind of general information are what author Robert Wegmann calls "switchboard people." They know the community and, like switchboard operators, can connect you with people or groups who can help you.

The next exercise will help you learn to identify switchboard people. Notice that sometimes your best bet is to go to the reference desk in the library. Other times you can visit or phone places like the chamber of commerce, YMCA, or stores for information.

Exercise 20:
Contact Sheet for Your Switchboard Network

Check off any contacts on this list that could have useful information about your leisure options. Then visit or phone them to get leads. Space is provided for writing in phone numbers, if you wish.

Top Leisure Resource Network List

☐ Library   _____

☐ Parks and Recreation Department   _____

☐ Travel, tourist, and visitor's bureaus   _____

☐ Chamber of Commerce   _____

☐ Retail outlets selling things used
in your leisure area of interest   _____

☐ Retail store with general community
and leisure knowledge (sports, hobby,
crafts, pets, garden, hardware)   _____

☐ YMCA, YWCA   _____

☐ AAA (auto)   _____

Additional Switchboard Contacts

☐ Career or counseling centers in local colleges

☐ Churches, synagogues, temples, or mosques

☐ County extension agents (often located at a college)

☐ Department of Transportation

☐ Department of Welfare, social workers

☐ Local media (newspaper, reporter with city desk or arts and leisure, radio and TV)

☐ Museums, fairgrounds, zoos, galleries, or cultural centers

☐ Voter registration or League of Women Voters, political parties

☐ Professional groups or associations, clubs, membership and service groups (Lions, Rotary)

☐ Scouts, Drug Education Resistance Education (DARE), youth groups

☐ Support groups (Alcoholics Anonymous, eating disorders, parents and singles' groups, groups advocating rights or recognition)

☐ Transportation services (bus, taxi, limousine, specialized services for people with disabilities)

☐ Union hall

☐ Volunteer bureau, RSVP, or United Way

Step 2: The Expert Interview

As you gather information about local people, resources, and opportunities, you'll probably come across the name of an expert in your area of interest. At this point, you can convert your general interest into a commitment, by meeting with this person. Through a survey or interview process, you'll gather insight and information which will deepen your understanding of where you want to go next. Thus, if you were interested in hot-air ballooning, you'd contact a person who enjoys floating across the sky. Hopefully, you'll be able to find an expert locally. If not, then try to find someone who has authored a book or article, presides over a national or regional organization, or volunteers their time in the area you're interested in. In today's well-connected world, you might even find your expert listed in a database, or on-line through e-mail and bulletin board postings. These days, you have many ways to do your interviewing—in person, by phone or modem, or, of course, by mail.

This step is called informational interviewing, and the technique has been borrowed from successful job-finding strategies. In the job search, you try to meet people who do the same kind of work you're interested in finding. Then, you simply reverse the job interview procedure by asking all the questions and actively listening.

As in a job interview, one must make an appointment and conduct oneself in a professional manner because you are asking for someone else's time and advice. Most job-seekers face this task with a degree of trepidation, asking, "Why would anyone want to talk with me; I'm unemployed." To their surprise, most people are happy to offer advice when they have the time. After all, the employee is being treated like a media star, being interviewed about something he or she does well—his or her job.

Many job-seekers report experiencing a magical moment when the employer (or person being interviewed) looks them over and asks, "Do you have a resumé?" If the line of questioning goes this way, the job-seeker knows that he or she has just developed a valuable contact. In this fashion, informational interviewing puts one in touch with valuable opportunities that normally aren't advertised in the want ads.

A leisure searcher shares the same basic goal. For instance, if you were interviewing a hot-air balloonist, you might ask the interviewer how he or she got started, what to bring along on a trip, how to select equipment, which magazines to read, and which clubs to join. And don't be surprised if the person you've just been treating as an expert rests a long, thoughtful gaze on you and says, "Say, if you're not busy next weekend, I'm taking out the rigging. Why don't you come along and see what it's like to float in a hot-air balloon gondola across the farms and fields?"

Once up among the clouds, you'll clearly see that you've made the right move. The ride and the leisure-search process are both exhilarating! Expert interviews frequently lead to unique experiences and collaborations.

Questions, Questions, Questions

After you decide to try the leisure search, you'll probably be scratching your head, wondering, "Yes, yes, but what kinds of questions should I ask?" Exercise 21 gives you a visual summary of the two-step process and the questions you might consider asking.

Exercise 21:
Leisure-Search Networking Steps and Questions

Review the two-step process. Then check off questions that are important to you.

Step 1: Collect contacts and general information

Switchboard People (People with General Information)

- Basic information (who does it, what, where, when, how much it costs)
- Tips & leads on classes, literature, and groups
- Names of local experts
- Brief personal contacts, can be done by phone

The Seven Beginning Questions

- ☐ 1. Where can I go to enjoy this leisure experience?
- ☐ 2. What can I read, view, or watch to learn more?
- ☐ 3. What classes can I take? How can I enroll?
- ☐ 4. What group could I join to learn more?
- ☐ 5. How much time does it take?
- ☐ 6. What are some of the costs?
- ☐ 7. Whom can I contact for expert advice?
- ☐ 8. Anyone else?

Step 2: Gather detailed information

Experts—People Who Can Give You:

- Tips for getting involved
- Creative solutions to problems
- Encouragement and support
- An in-person interview or demonstration

Sample Questions

General Warm-up Questions

- ☐ How did you get started in this area? Did anybody help?
- ☐ When did you first get started?
- ☐ How long does it take to learn the basics?
- ☐ How long does it take to master the more advanced skills?
- ☐ What do you enjoy most about this activity?
- ☐ What do you find most routine or what do you like least?

Leisure Style and Preferences

- ☐ How many hours a week do you spend doing this?
- ☐ How do you prefer to learn new skills: books, classes, self-teaching, friends?
- ☐ Do you usually enjoy doing this activity alone or with others?
- ☐ Are most of the people involved in this similar in age, gender, and background, or are they all pretty different?
- ☐ About how much money do you spend each week on this activity?
- ☐ Do your leisure skills and interests relate to your work skills and interests?
- ☐ Do you know anyone who turned their leisure interest into a business or a job?
- ☐ If you could change your leisure life what might you do differently?

Specific Recommendations

- ☐ Can you recommend any books, magazines, catalogs, or cassettes?
- ☐ Would you recommend any classes or joining a club?
- ☐ What are some low-cost ways of getting started?
- ☐ How could I get started in this leisure area?
- ☐ Could you recommend another person I could talk to?

Networking Tips

The bounty of information you receive will flow directly from the quality of your networking efforts. Most of the time, you will begin by talking to people you know. With a bit of confidence, you will branch out to switchboard people. Here, too, you can draw a lesson from successful job-seekers. Your networking will be most effective when you contact people beyond your circle of friends and acquaintances. Reaching out to total strangers pays big dividends.

One famous job-search study found that people who had networked with strangers for their jobs made an average of $2,500 per year more than those who confined their networking contacts to people they knew. The cardinal networking principal is that your greatest rewards will often come from your weakest connections.

Winning Network Techniques

What is the best way to approach a person? What's the best opener? The answers to these and other common questions will be presented next in the form of a script worksheet that allows you to write your own script, rehearse it, and then go off to collect your leisure leads and tips.

In the first part, you'll learn to always start with an introduction in order to bridge the barrier of talking with a stranger. Your introduction needs to communicate your purpose so the expert knows why he or she is being interviewed.

Instead of asking for answers to your questions, try asking for advice. Ask not for the exact location of a great fishing spot, but whom you might contact to find out about great fishing holes. This indirect approach makes it easier for the other person to respond. They don't have to come up with precise answers, nor divulge information to a stranger. As a result, you come away with better quality information.

Finally, be sure to ask for the names of two other people to contact. Otherwise, how will your network grow if you don't continually find new seeds from which to sprout new contacts?

Exercise 22:
Networking Tips and Script Worksheet

Getting advice from people is a skill shared by successful reporters, detectives, researchers, politicians, and job-hunters. National surveys show that people who network for job leads will find work sooner than those who just read job advertisements. The same can probably be said for "leisure hunters." Here are three steps that successful networkers use. Read through each step and fill in the blanks with your own ideas. This will help you master what you'll need to know. Later, you'll learn some more tips to add to the steps. Read each tip and then write a focus statement under each one.

Tip #1: Introduce yourself *and* your purpose.

Introductions are especially important on the phone. Don't make a general request, like, "Do you know how I could get involved in wordworking?" Instead, tell them what you are looking for. Then ask for advice or information, "I'm new in town and I'm looking for information about where wood carvers might meet or be found. Can you suggest someone to contact?"

Write your possible opener for a phone call here:

_____

_____

Tip #2: Don't ask for answers—ask for advice.

People love to be asked advice, but they usually don't like to be put on the spot and have to come up with specific answers. Therefore, don't ask them, "Where can I go to join a woodcarver's club?" Instead ask for advice, "Do you know anyone or any place I might visit to find out about local woodcarvers in Olympia?"

Write your possible key request for advice here:

_____

_____

_____

Tip #3: Try to get two additional names (leads for future contacts).

Never walk away empty-handed. By always asking for the names of other people to contact, you'll collect clues that will lead to the next step. You may want to carry a small paper or electronic notebook for recording your leads.

What might you say to solicit more leads?

_____

_____

_____

Rehearse and Practice

Rehearse your script until you're confident. Then practice by networking with three to five people about your least important leisure interests. Try to approach strangers or people you don't know well. See what tips you come up with. Then practice by asking other people for advice about one of the leisure interests you hold dear to your heart. Don't be surprised if you find people helpful and advice plentiful.

Networking Example

Scott Etlinger wanted to find out about hot-air ballooning opportunities in a town he had never lived in: Olympia, Washington.
By using telephone networking techniques only, Scott hit pay dirt
in just seventy-five minutes. His three most productive contacts
are noted by a star. Scott found the names of places to get a ride
and three national organizations. Notice that Scott got good results
from calling the library as well as contacting organizations with
switchboard people (airport personnel). Note also that many contacts led nowhere.

1. Parks and Recreation Department—Olympia

First Set of Leads
⇩

   1. Puyallup Valley ⇨   Referrals from Leads
   ⇩   ⇩

   2. Seattle Visitor   2a. Twin County
      Center   Chamber of Commerce
                              (see below)

     ⇩   ⇩

   3. Olympia Visitor ⇨ 3a. No referrals from ⇨ Referrals from
      Convention Bureau   Visitor Bureau   Referrals
                            ⇩   ⇩

                        3a. Olympia Airport   3b. Mr. George Y.
                                              (not in)

2. Twin County Chamber of Commerce

   ☆ Air fair at Chehalis Airport

3. Tourist and Visitor Bureau—Olympia/Thurston

   1. Visitor Center of Olympia
   2. Twin County Chamber of Commerce

4. Sporting Goods Stores

   1. Olympic Outfitters⇨ 1a. Olympia Airport ⇨ 1b. Library
                      1a. PacWest
                            ⇩

   2. Rainbow Sports   2a. Olympia Airport

5. Library—Olympia
  ☆ Balloons Federation of America
  ☆ High America Balloon
  ☆ Sport Balloons Assoc. of the United States of America

6. YMCA and YWCA

Olympia Parks ⇨   Olympia Chamber ⇨ ☆ Tacoma phone
and Recreation   of Commerce   book under
                                            "Hot Air Balloons"

7. AAA (travel club)
  ☆ Balloon Rides, Tacoma, Go Lightly, Inc.

Evaluating and Expanding Your Network Techniques

Were you surprised at what you found out in the previous network exercise? Most people pick up tips and leads quite easily. Eventually, you'll come to realize that this truly is the information age and that there are vast quantities of useful information floating just below the surface. Once you begin to scratch that surface with networking questions, you will be amazed at how close you are standing to the answers you need.

Evaluate your techniques by rating yourself on these three skills:

• I remembered to introduce myself.
• I only requested advice.
• I always asked for another network lead.

You can improve your networking skills by adding four advanced techniques to your repertoire:

• Use a referral's name.
• Tell why you value this person's help.
• Make your contact feel comfortable while they stop to think and recall useful information.
• Ask permission to check back.

One quality stands out above all else among winning job seekers: perseverance. In the hot-air ballooning example, most people would give up phoning after three dead-end calls. By persisting, Scott was able to succeed. You may have to endure several empty contacts before you find one truly fruitful one.

Exercise 23:
Advanced Network Tips

Examine these advanced tips and decide which ones you would like to use. You may have already begun to incorporate some of them, but this activity will make you fully aware of your networking skills.

Tip #1: Use your previous contact's name.

Mention the previous contact person who gave you the name of the person you are now talking to. This converts your status from stranger to potential friend. You become somebody who shares a common acquaintance.

"Jessica said you might have some information about ceramics."

☐ I've done this before.   ☐ I want to try this one next time.

Tip #2: Tell why you think the person can help.

People are more likely to help you when you make them feel special.

"Jessica mentioned the craft booth you once ran at the Farmer's Market."

☐ I've done this before.   ☐ I want to try this one next time.

Tip #3: Give the person a chance to think.

After asking the question, pause, and give the person a chance to think. Wait patiently or make some small talk. It could sound something like this:

Any advice you have about fishing spots would be great. (pause) I just moved into town. I used to live in Eastern Washington. The fishing back there was great. I've heard that the fishing here is different. I can't wait to catch a rainbow trout. I've heard they can put up a good fight.

☐ I've done this before.   ☐ I want to try this one next time.

Tip #4: Ask to check back.

You may want to use this tip if your request is about an unusual topic. Checking back gives people a chance to think; it's a very effective technique in developing job-hunting leads. When you ask permission to check back, you let the person know that you are serious. As a result, your contact is more likely to treat your request for advice seriously.

☐ I've done this before.   ☐ I want to try this one next time.

Community Exploration: The Final Leisure-Search Task

You and I have now arrived at the moment of truth. It is time to back your desire for leisure wellness up with the necessary actions. You must temporarily put down the book and actually go out and visit, phone, read, or network in order to gather the information you need.

Your leisure search now begins in earnest. All the previous exercises—brainstorming, journal writing, surveys, and inventories—have brought us to this final step leading out to the community. It is time to begin applying the techniques outlined in this chapter.

As you leave these pages and step out into the community, your search will provide you with a new source of energy, which launches you onto a new and more fulfilling leisure pathway.

The moment of truth is at hand.

The leisure-search strategy chart in Exercise 24 will help you plot your first steps. Some people find the written goal very compelling. For others, the written word and the strategic plan are nothing more than scratches on a page. The journal exercises are included to help you reach beyond my words and tap into the words in your heart. It doesn't matter whether you prefer writing goals or journals, mulling things over, or waiting for inspiration—you must understand that you are standing on the launching pad. Your new leisure ethic will either take flight or crash and burn amidst the words on this page.

Please consider setting aside some time over the next one to two weeks for the purpose of conducting your leisure search. You might find everything you need in that period—or you may need to continue the search later. Setting aside the time now is the most important behavior change you'll ever make.

As you discover hidden opportunities and talk with encouraging and exciting people, you'll discover that the leisure search is as healthy as jogging, and as essential as working. The search process reinforces the habit of life-long learning because it translates the learning act into a practical and essential step towards wellness. A new dream can be born from your leisure-search efforts.

In summary, whether you use the following planning exercise, or not, the actual exploration of your community is what comes next—and it counts for everything!

Remember Marshall McLuhan's observation that, "When all is said and done, more will be said than done." Hopefully, you will take time out now to insure that when all is read and done, more will be done than was read.

Developing a Leisure-Search Strategy

Unsuccessful job seekers often use a random hit-or-miss approach. Some days they look for work for two or three hours, and other days zero hours. But every prosperous business, and every triumphant job seeker, follows a strategy or plan. Success follows from the disciplined effort of methodically gathering information, following up on leads, and persisting in the face of adversity.

Since this is a leisure search, we need to recast the language and compare it to a scavenger hunt. Regardless of the words or labels used, you'll arrive at your goal or destination more quickly if you plan your work and work your plan.

To help you chart and record a plan, use the following scavenger-hunt chart. This chart lists the different sources of information and summarizes your findings. It can also be used to log or record your efforts. A sample chart follows, illustrating how it might look when filled out. To make this chart work for you, set a goal of finding one tidbit of information in each of the five areas. Then summarize your efforts with a journal session.

Exercise 24:
Charting Your Leisurely Scavenger Hunt

The charts on pages 145 and 146 will help you plot your leisure-search strategy. Like a job search, the leisure search begins by listing leads, or possible opportunities. Network! Ask others for ideas, just as you would in a job search. Record your leads in the left-hand column. As you begin to investigate and gather specific ideas, record new information and ideas to follow up on in the right-hand column. You can add to either column at any time. As you begin completing both columns, you'll find yourself filling the empty places in your leisure lifestyle.

Exercise 25:
Leisure Journal Assignment:
Summarizing the Leisure Search

Summarize what you did during your leisure search. Did you read, talk to friends, make phone calls, visit stores, network, or chat with switchboard people?

_____

_____

_____

What was the most interesting thing you learned from people, the media, or books?

_____

_____

_____

Leisure Search Strategy Chart

Leads—findings and people or places to contact	To follow up on next
1. To read or view or write List things to read (books, magazines, newsletters, brochures) or view (video, CD-ROM, slides, software, etc.), and organizations to write to for more information. ——————— ——————— ———————	
2. To see or visit List groups, clubs, associations, events, and conferences. ——————— ——————— ———————	
3. To enroll in or find out about Classes, workshops, and training events. ——————— ——————— ——————— ———————	
4. To interview Experts. ——————— ——————— ———————	

Sample Leisure Search Strategy Chart: Hot Air Ballooning

This sample chart will help you visualize how your leisure search might be recorded.

Leads—findings and people or places to contact	To follow up on next
1. *To read or view or write* Find out about ballooning magazines from library. Look for ads for videotapes and books. Look for ads for rides in Yellow Pages. Write to National Balloonist Assn.	No books, but one magazine. Lots of ads for rides. One offered a workshop, see vol. #4–1993
2. *To see or visit* Visit airport and talk to pilots. Network to find the names of balloonists.	Airport man—call Tacoma airfield. Someone mentioned Ted Aleron, who once took a balloon out. Teaches at local school.
3. *To enroll in or find out about* See if any shows or events are scheduled. Call local Parks and Recreation Dept.	Go to hot-air baloon fair in Seattle. Ask about helping out in set-up in exchange for a ride.
4. *To interview* Experts.	

Reflect on one barrier, frustration, or problem you encountered.

_____

_____

_____

Write about any new ideas or feelings of renewal and excitement you may have experienced.

_____

_____

_____

What will you do next?

_____

_____

CHAPTER 7

A Leisurely Summation

N THIS FINAL chapter, you and I will weave together the various strands or themes that make up the pursuit of serious play. We'll celebrate your efforts and reflect upon your attitude and use of time—and on the metaphor "leisure is time's treasure chest." Hopefully, new horizons will beckon to you as you become more serious about your playfulness and your leisure time.

The Passage of Time

Time still remains an enigma for many people (including the author). Humanity has responded to this puzzle with precision, rather than poetry. Our societies are pre-occupied with measuring time by using clocks and charts. We delight in the new electronic gadgets dedicated to digitizing every last second, tracking our phone contacts, and scheduling our lives.

Stop and ponder the mystery.
Stop and look at your wrist watch.

Gaze upon the advancing numbers,
the never-tiring army of minutes
parading endlessly by ...

Each second counted—then sent off into the void

Perhaps that wrist watch is an illusion, making it appear as if time were a thing. The various scheduling devices and calendars (personal digital assistants, Franklin Planners, Day Timers, etc.) further delude us into thinking that time is something we can control or conquer.

Time Is a Subjective Experience

The intertwining dance of *time, space,* and *speed* was first formulated by Albert Einstein. He described a situation where time and space are relative to the speed or tempo of your dance (especially when dancing at the speed of light). Perhaps, Einstein's hypothesis can open a door on our perception of leisure time. We can apply his notion that one's sense of time is relative to each person's unique position.

Our songs and poetry often refer to time as a "flowing river." The perception of the river's speed depends on where one stands. Children, playing in the shallows, see the river of time very differently than adults. A child's total and spontaneous involvement keeps him or her keenly aware of the present moment, but blissfully ignorant of past and future.

Unlike children, adults are more attuned to the passage of time. Perhaps it is because age brings with it a basic awareness of one's finite and mortal nature. Adults immersed in a leisure activity find that time seems to either speed up or slow down. Thumbing through pictures of last year's vacation, you casually toss out the words, "It seems so long ago ..." Time seems to have slowed, with a giant distance separating past from present

Later, when the playful children have grown up and gone off to college, you're again glancing through a photo album of vacation pictures. Again, looking at last year's vacation, you're overheard to say, "I can remember that trip as if we had just gone last week." This time the distance between yesterday and today seems to have shrunk. These examples demonstrate how the passage of time or time itself may, in fact, be a human construct or invention.

If you pause to examine the pace of life today, you might conclude that we are "living lives of speed." This is particularly true for people with extensive or complicated family responsibilities like single parents, dual wage earners managing households, and those supporting extended families. Many people feel like a hamster running in an exercise wheel. Their lives are constantly filled with "doing, doing, doing." One advertising agency translated this common experience into a marketing slogan for Nike shoes with the slogan: "Just do it."™

Jean-Louis Servan-Schreiber, the author of *The Art of Time* writes, "The notion of reflection has vanished into very thin air. We make decisions in a flash, intuitively rather than deliberately and reflectively.... We become sprinters of action, we lack the wind for the long-distance race of reflection." He feels that the over-emphasis on acting or doing results in losing the ability to concentrate, and suggests that people need to consciously insert more pauses or time for reflection into their daily routine.

Following this advice, it is essential that you stop and reflect about time and the experience of time. Try taking a little time out of each day to reflect, to take in all that is happening and sense the entire landscape of your experience. This pause will help you feel that your life is less raggedy, and that your hand is perhaps a bit more firmly planted on the steering wheel of your life's vessel.

Examining Time—The Experience of Doing Nothing

In the next exercise you will be asked to stop everything and try to do nothing for twenty minutes. This experience requires that you try to enter a semi-meditative state where your mind is cleared and you merely observe and experience the present moment you inhabit. This is an invaluable exercise for everyone, and especially workaholics.

Whatever you do, you should not make phone calls, review things you have to do, think about work or obligations to others, or ponder personal problems. This is not a time to chat and visit with others. It is a solitary moment for a talk with yourself. It is a chance to relax, take in some deep breaths and exhale deep feelings or thoughts.

You will only be successful at this exercise if you grant yourself permission to do nothing.... This may be a tough assignment

for people with a strong Protestant work ethic—where leisure is often suspect. Begin by personally defining what "doing nothing" means for you. At the very least, it must become a commitment to a moment of *un*committed time ... trying to experience time without a goal or purpose.

You may choose to try and clear your mind of all thoughts, as in a meditative trance. Or, you might prefer daydreaming about a time in your life—or time itself. You may wish to go off and gaze at clouds, stroll through a park, or sit in a garden. This exercise is almost impossible to do wrong if you try and stay in the present moment of unobligated free time.

If you find your mind meandering over to the topic of work or your to-do list, gently remind yourself to relax and look about you. Ask yourself, "What do I see about me? What do I want to get out of this moment of free time?" When you arrive at the end of the twenty minutes, you'll write a reflective piece about time leisure. Additional directions for this experience and the reflective journal assignment are given in the next exercise.

Exercise 26:
Leisure Journal Assignment: Leisure and Time Reflection
During the first twenty minutes ...

- Try to do nothing for at least twenty minutes ...
  Doing nothing could include: Daydreaming, meditating,

watching people, sitting back, strolling aimlessly, watching clouds, observing insects, or staring at the hairs on your hand.

- Be alone ... away from others who may distract you ...
- Have no goals, avoid conversation, just be ...
- Try to experience time.
  Try to be in the moment.
  Think about time.
- Look around.
  Look into yourself ...
- Stare at your watch.
  Stare at your life.
  Stare at this page ...

After about twenty minutes, answer as many of these questions as you can ... on another piece of paper.

1. What are your thoughts after twenty minutes of trying to do nothing?
2. What is one thing you want to remember about this experience with "time"?
3. What do the words "leisure wellness" mean to you?

How will you answer these questions ...

4. What would you like your leisure to be like one year from today?
5. What is one beginning step you can take to change the quality of your leisure life? What is one small thing you can change?

Consider Your Ability to Do Nothing

How did you react to twenty minutes of trying to do nothing? Was it easy or challenging? When you sit and do nothing at home, do you feel guilty or anxious? Do family members complain about how much work you do? Do you feel uncomfortable if you're not busy? Would you rather help organize events so you don't have to sit around and talk to people?

Consider the findings of a Hilton Hotel study which revealed that 90 percent of Americans spend almost half their weekend doing chores or working at their jobs.

How do you react to an extra hour in the fall, when the clocks are set behind sixty minutes? My wife, Judy, thinks about that extra hour for weeks prior, relishing the thought.

Unfortunately, not all of us are as well prepared to enjoy those extra moments. Sometimes, when we run into unexpected free time, we find ourselves partnered with boredom or anxiety. One author suggests that becoming uneasy or "fidgeting" during the experience of free time is often a product of the extra time combined with extra energy. You can eliminate your anxiety when you accept two facts. First, you do not always need to be productive every moment of your time. Second, it often takes practice or a conscious effort to enjoy unplanned free time.

The secret lies in choosing small, easy-to-do activities (or a moment of inactivity) which brings you pleasure. Use the following five tips to turn unexpected free moments at work, during commuting, or at home into healthy leisure moments.

1. Simply observe what is going on around you. Look out a window at the sky and notice the weather. Look at your desk, or examine a wallet photo.

2. Take a deep breath, and pay attention to your breathing.

3. Examine posture, how can you change it or relax it.

4. Take a stroll, or at least daydream.

5. If you enjoy people, visit with someone about their weekend plans. Try complimenting them on something you enjoy about them.

You can profit from this twenty minute experiment in "doing nothing" only if you become more aware of the choices you make. To deepen this experiment, imagine that you had grown up during that part of human history where the average person did not own a clock. In this pre-industrial setting, you might gauge time by the organic rhythms and clues provided by nature. The perception of time would necessitate observations about light and the position of the sun and stars in the sky. Temperature and the smells of animals and plants would provide clues. Scheduling would be by season rather than by digital readouts. To re-acquaint yourself with this organic form of time-telling, try the following two things:

1. On Saturday or in the evening go around without a watch.

2. Remind yourself that it is not humanly possible to make every minute count in terms of productivity or responsibility. Take moments out and try to do nothing for five minutes. De-accelerate *because acceleration is addicting.*

The Leisure Moments Credit Card

As previously noted, the way you use your small spare moments is a good barometer for your leisure wellness. While we often plan how to enjoy the longer periods spanning weekends and vacations, the use or abuse of short moments defines the texture of our leisure.

Season the hectic pace of modern life with a delicious pause. Invest yourself creatively in a small moment. When you're in a traffic jam play your favorite music, sing, or join in with a musical instrument. I play my blues harmonica at long torturous stoplights. As you wait in line, day dream or become a camera lens observing the details. Take a moment out on the commute home to drive through the car wash. As the car proceeds, close your eyes and pretend you're in a submarine. Even though it costs a little time and some money, you can pause a minute and are one chore ahead for the weekend. Spending time or money in this way is not foolish—it is nourishing. It is the art of serious play.

To help you focus on these small bits of time, copy the Leisure Moments Credit Card, fill it in, and put it in your wallet next to your credit card. This will remind you that while money is renewable, your time is not. Think of the Leisure Moments Credits Card as a prescription of small time pills, used to remedy burn out, stress, and even depression.

If you review this card daily for two weeks, it just might remind you of the importance of the motto: Play Now or Pay Later.

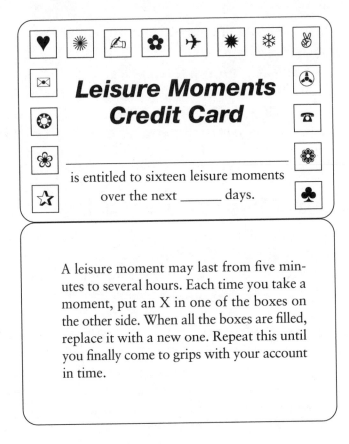

A leisure moment may last from five minutes to several hours. Each time you take a moment, put an X in one of the boxes on the other side. When all the boxes are filled, replace it with a new one. Repeat this until you finally come to grips with your account in time.

What Should I Do Next?

This book is packed with suggestions. However, it would be a mistake to try and change all of your leisure habits and values at once. Successful change is based on making change by degrees. You may start with nothing more than decreasing one behavior such as television watching. The result of this effort is an increase in free time which you might use for journal writing, reading, cooking a gourmet meal, or strolling about the neighborhood.

The principle of moderation applies to starting a new leisure interest. For example, if you want to take up a new sport like golf, begin by driving by the golf course on your way home. The next step might include parking nearby, observing, and visualizing yourself on the course. Think about where you might rent or borrow clubs. Eventually, you'll get a magazine subscription, and make your first commitment in terms of time and money. Finally, you plan for a day when you can accompany a friend across the greens. At the end of the day you sign up for a class. As you make each change, you experience an increasing exhilaration and confidence about moving off of dead center onto a new leisure pathway.

In essence, you are not being asked to fill your already crowded (or empty) life with a lot of *shoulds*—I should avoid wearing a watch on Saturday, I should network with the grocer, I should . . . I should do more of this and less of that. *Shoulds* can turn the pursuit of serious play into the vice of serious guilt.

To illustrate the importance of this message, suppose you are on vacation at a beautiful lake resort. It is thirty minutes until dinner is served in the main dining hall. You have brought along a racy novel, which you started last week at home. Now you face a dilemma. Should you stroll around the lake before dinner or sit and read the trashy book? You remember the lessons of this book and assume that you might be wasting your precious leisure time reading a book, which can be done at any time back home.

Before you decide what to do with the extra thirty minutes, review your definition of leisure. If it includes the idea that leisure is an attitude and not an activity, then you will be guided in a certain direction. Your definition of leisure will tell you that your attitude about what you are doing, during this moment before dinner, is what matters most. Your most nurturing act might very well be the reading of this book. Leisure wellness has no room for guilt!

The final exercise will help you pinpoint more clearly what you expect from a healthy dose of serious play. The exercise will assist you in banishing the voice of guilt, while tuning into the beckoning whisper of leisure wellness.

Exercise 27:
Leisure Journal Assignment:
Your Leisure Bill of Rights

In 1978 Dr. C. Forrest McDowell wrote one of the first *Leisure Bills of Rights*. The one on this page is adapted from his book *Leisure Wellness* and is reprinted with his permission.

Review *The Leisure Bill of Rights* and then respond to the questions at the end of this exercise.

You have the right to remain silent and introspective while you read your leisure rights.

The Leisure Bill of Rights

The right to do nothing. This includes the right to pause in the middle of a hectic schedule, to find value in doing nothing. It includes the right to pursue activities like contemplation and day-dreaming.

The right to procrastinate. While this right has limits, it includes the choice to do something outside of your obligations in order to regain a sense of control in a busy life-schedule.

The right to be uncertain. This includes the choice to experience time without always having a plan.

The right to be alone. This includes the right to journey inwards into your own space and time, while respecting the needs of others.

The right to be playful or childlike. This is based on giving yourself permission to act spontaneously, humorously, and sometimes strangely. It also gives you permission to indulge in asking curious questions, abandoning yourself in play, wondering and wandering, and other childlike behaviors.

The right to self-expression. It is the right to dabble, to explore, to try new things while realizing that you are the final judge of their worth. It implies that you may engage in any activity without judging it by professional standards.

Write your own Leisure Bill of Rights.

  1. Copy over the ones you like from above.

  2. Add to these by creating your own rights.

  3. Copy your own Leisure Bill of Rights onto parchment and place it in an important place.

Your Second Leisure Wellness Score

In the first chapter you completed a pre-test or inventory of your own leisure wellness entitled: #3 *The Kimeldorf Leisure Wellness Survey.* At this point, it might be useful to review your original answers and note any changes you might make at this time. This final review will help you gain a sense of growth. You are not asked to take the test again because that would suggest that your leisure wellness can be precisely measured like cholesterol or calories. Rest assured, you have improved your leisure wellness by the very act of reaching this page in the book.

As you reconsider your responses to the wellness survey, consider what kind of future leisure choices you will be making over the next year. Hopefully your choices will improve the quality of your leisure life. Then promise to return to this survey one year from now to sound the depths of change.

Quality Leisure Time

Witold Rybczynski, author of *Waiting for the Weekend,* quizzes his readers with this question, "How did we come to divide our lives into a rigorous schedule of five days of work, followed by two days play?" He notes that this work and weekend routine is not based on organic cycles of our moon, seasons, or the Earth's rotation.

And yet, this cycle of several work days followed by a holiday or weekend is found in several cultures. Jewish people celebrate the Sabbath every seventh day, Mohammed and the early Christians chose a holy day each week (Saturday and Friday). This oscillation of work-and-weekend makes work the routine and play the interruption.

Like many human constructs, this artifice has been left unexamined for far too long. Our over-scheduled culture has arrived at a point where free time seems unnatural ... even uninviting. As a result, some of us must carry around Leisure Moment Credit Cards just to remind us to engage in divine moments of play.

As you finish this last chapter, carefully consider the words of one journalist who wrote, "The problem may not be as simple as the scarcity or abundance of free time. It is more likely that we face the problem of finding too little meaning in our existing free time." Servan-Schreiber, author of *The Art of Time*, builds on this viewpoint when he points out how mastery of our time ultimately rests upon mastery of ourselves. We can only take control of our time once we know what we want to do with it. Hopefully, as you close this book you have many more ideas of what you want from the time you have left.

"So, What Do You Do?"

REMIND MYSELF THAT the greatest lessons spring from the smallest kernels of existence. As a workaholic, I must remind myself to make an effort to open time's treasure chest just a bit more each day. I try to dig more deeply through the jewels known to me as my leisure moments.

Moreover, when I am at a party and someone asks, "What do you do?" I will no longer limit myself by reciting my job title, "I'm a teacher." Instead, I hope to have the wisdom of offering a more balanced reply, "Besides teaching, I also enjoy writing, painting, practicing magic, and playing my harmonica." In this way, I reinforce the notion that I am the sum of both my work and my play.

THIS IS NOT a complete listing on the subject of leisure, but it includes many titles and authors referred to in this book.

Bolles, Richard. *The Three Boxes of Life.* Berkeley: Ten Speed Press, 1981. An outstanding discussion of balancing work, leisure, and education.

Career Planning and Adult Development Journal 5, no. 2 (1989). This issue, entitled "Work/ Leisure Connection," and edited by Martin Kimeldorf, contains seven articles discussing the work-leisure connection from several angles (retirement, education, expanding the definition of work).

Career Planning and Adult Development Journal 7, no. 2 (1991). This issue, entitled "Leisure-Hidden Tools for Life Planning and Development," and edited by Patsy B. Edwards and Martin Kimeldorf, contains nine articles exploring the different ways leisure relates to counseling, productivity, intergenerational approaches to ageism, religion, community service, politics, and self-esteem.

Chapman, Elwood. *Comfort Zones: Planning Your Future.* Menlo Park, Calif.: Crisp Publications, 1990.

———. *Enhance Your Destiny.* Menlo Park, Calif.: Crisp Publications, 1991. Chapman is a leader in retirement and senior life planning. His books are highly motivating.

Davidson, Jeff. *Breathing Space.* New York: Multimedia, 1991. If you are facing too many demands on your time, this book will help you understand the "megatrends" that may be victimizing you. The author provides some very original tools for creating more breathing space in personal, professional, and home life.

Faulkner, Rozanne W. *Therapeutic Recreation Protocol for Treatment of Substance Addictions.* State College, Pa.: Venture

Publishing, Inc., 1991. A fascinating description of how leisure education and therapeutic recreation can be utilized in a treatment setting for people trying to overcome addictions.

Godbey, Geoffrey. *Leisure In Your Life*. 3d ed. State College, Pa.: Venture Publishing, Inc., 1990. A good introduction to the field of leisure education.

Kimeldorf, Martin, and Howard Kimeldorf. "Work, Education, and the Quality of Life: Reconsidering Some Twentieth Century Myths." *International Journal of Career Management* 24, no. 4 (1993). This journal is devoted to the decline in the value and importance of work, family, and education. It examines the high tech myth against the low-tech reality we endure every day.

Rybczynski, Witold. *Waiting for the Weekend*. New York: Viking Penguin, 1991. An insightful study into the evolution of leisure and our weekend lifestyle.

Schore, Juliet B. *The Overworked American* New York: Harper-Collins, 1992. This seminal work examines how the unequal (and at times irrational) distribution of work and time affects our quality of life.

Servan-Schreiber, Jean-Louis. *The Art of Time*. Reading, Mass.: Addison-Wesley Publishing Co., Inc., 1988. This is a very provocative piece about time and managing time.

von Oech, Roger. *A Whack on the Side of the Head*. New York: Warner Books, 1990. This best-selling book provides useful techniques for stimulating creative thought. If you get stuck while working out your leisure alternatives, consult this book for problem-solving methods that work.

Wilson, Steve. *The Art of Mixing Work and Play*. Reynoldsburg, Ohio: Advocate Publishing Group, 1992. The author offers many insights into the value and role of humor and play in the work site.

Works in Progress

Kimeldorf, Martin. *Looking for Leisure In All the Right Places*. This student workbook explores the concepts of *Serious Play* for young adults in a curricular format designed for schools and community groups.

————. *Write to the Core.* This book contains over 100 innovative journal writing techniques based on the author's thirty years of keeping diaries. Learn how to turn a journal into a counselor-friend, scrapbook of your life story, or a special archive for your life's many passages. Learn how journal writing can become both fun and meaningful, even if you've never, ever written one word on a journal page before.

Million Dollar Idea #1: Senior Master's Degree

N YOUR FIRST CAREER, the most important question was, "What do I want to be when I grow up?" This simple yet provocative question reemerges as you enter your second career, your retirement, and the following information shows how to design a short-term learning program that can help people plan for their post-retirement second career.

Dubbed the Senior Master's Degree program, it is modeled after graduate level college programs in which students develop a project (thesis) based on an area of intense personal interest. Similarly, in this endeavor, seniors use their previous knowledge and information-gathering skills to research and investigate the thesis. The product of that endeavor helps guide them in designing a *second* career plan. Participants need not have previously graduated from college, but they *do* need a desire to keep learning about life and their mission. Graduates earn a "Master's degree" which acknowledges their senior status and honors the wisdom and vision that come with age and continued self-study.

Success in one's first career is dependent on the interweaving of three crucial ingredients: preparation, experience, and critical career thinking. Preparation usually begins with school and continues through life in the form of workshops and seminars. Experience comes from actual working, guidance from mentors, and pursuit of role models. Critical career thinking usually centers on taking stock of one's current career achievements, pondering career change, and making plans for acquiring more skills through promotions or formal schooling opportunities.

These three ingredients play out in the second career, but with a slight twist on each one. Preparation must now be done in a foreshortened mode. One may not have the time, resources, or stamina to return to a formal multiyear college-level program. My proposed model is built around formal training that could take place on a "campus" twice a year for two periods lasting approximately two weeks each. The remainder of the learning is self-directed and is completed by the student back in his or her community. In this way, the program involves minimal costs in terms of time and dollars. The second factor, experience, takes on a new dimension, as students can draw upon a lifetime of incredibly valuable experience and skill. Consequently, the last ingredient changes from critical career thinking to *reflective* career thinking. It is time to sum up, assess, and redefine one's career in the broadest terms possible.

In this fashion, the word "career" returns to the original meaning: path or course. The student is trying to define his or her mission in a world no longer limited to paid forms of work. One must consider his or her total career needs across many domains: paid work (permanent, temporary, freelance, consulting, business), unpaid forms of "work" (volunteering, self-study, schooling, hobbies), serious play (the art of doing nothing, humor, playfulness, balance). Other important factors may include family, spiritual, health, and general wellness. As such, the distinction between work and play is no longer important. What *is* important is the discovery of a new (perhaps final) mission and the passionate pursuit of it across the different stages of the second career—from young senior to elder senior.

The Senior Master's Degree curriculum is centered on the subject of one's second career. The goal is for each student to graduate with a personal strategic blueprint outlining what could be called a second career plan. The course of study includes:

- the stages in a second career
- opportunities for both work and leisure
- financial and survival strategies
- methods for sustaining and promoting physical and mental wellness

- personal life-story writing (journal, secular or spiritual autobiographies, memoirs) which helps sum up the journey to the present point in time.

In this curriculum, students assess their first career experiences and plan for their second career trajectory. They develop this planning against a background awareness of the changes they will likely experience as they grow older. Personal goals are sketched out against probable changes in physical and mental health, finances, and other developmental issues of aging.

Students will gather twice a year on a campus for about one week each time. The campus could involve dormitories in a college, a state park with residential or camping and meeting facilities, or a local community or senior center. During the two weeks, first-year students enroll in short courses conducted in a workshop or seminar format (this is not the time for lectures). Teachers are assisted by second-year students who share their experiences from the previous year. In this way, second-year students become role models or mentors.

In the second year, students develop an informal project or thesis which defines the mission for their second career. When they have completed their independent research and planning, they report back to the school to answer the question, "What do you want to do, now that you're grown up?" Their answer is presented as a culminating project which is shared with the entire school, prior to graduation. Students can keep in touch with professors during the year via phone and interactive computer networks. They leave connected with other people who have similar passions, values, and interests. As a result, they do not have to enter their second career alone, confused, angry, or forgotten.

They graduate and leave the program with a Senior Master's Degree. It recognizes their accomplishments of the past and promise for the future. This final certificate is not just a degree. It becomes their formal invitation to renewal. The details of this curriculum for total life-long learning follows.

Curriculum Overview

The following is an overview of the curriculum. It begins with a narrative describing each semester and is followed by a syllabus listing for the coursework and sequence.

First Semester

First semester students enroll in a one-week residential, basic core curriculum. They study the developmental life-stages of the second career, which typically begins after mid life and extends into the later years. They study the essential challenge and options which present themselves at different phases of the second career. Then students identify options for utilizing and exploring their talents across three domains: paid work, leisure, and community service. This core curriculum also provides students with information and techniques for summing up a first career and planning a second career. Thus, the curriculum serves as a transition from first to second career. Students leave the first semester core curriculum with the mission of deciding how they want to spend their time during the second career in the areas of leisure, community service, and paid forms of work. After choosing all or one of the areas to explore in their home town they return in six months for a one-week second semester meeting.

Second Semester

In the second session, students review their work and progress. They enroll in three more quick technique courses covering various forms of wellness, financial planning and survival tips, and methods for summing up their first career. They review goals which must be met by the time they return to the campus for their final sequence of classes. When they return they need to turn in a product summing up their first career (journal, scrapbook, autobiography, portfolio, etc.), develop an initial plan for their second career, and gather detailed information about home town opportunities. Thus, the product they create tells about their accomplishments and experiences in their first career, outlines a goal for using their talents during their time during their second career, and compiles a list of local agencies, businesses, clubs, associations, or books which contain information about their second career goals.

Third Semester

In the first semester of the second year, returning students share what they have learned with new first-year students. They become teaching assistants, mentors or adjunct professors in the college. While not teaching and sharing, they are working on the final details of their second career plan and completing work on a final presentation of their culminating project—which will be presented to the entire faculty and study body. A checklist-type contract is used to mark the completion of their final project.

Fourth Semester

In the final semester of the second year, students present their final project . If it is not ready, they may use this time to work on completing the project and present it at the next semester. This culminating activity serves as a role model and as a special rite of passage to a second career. Once the project is satisfactorily completed the student receives a Senior Master's Degree with the option of returning to contribute as an adjunct professor in the future.

Core Curriculum ... Year 1

Semester #1—Basics

Life Planning for Your Second Career
Study the developmental issues of aging and identify new passions, dreams, and goals for the second half of life.

Leisure Wellness (Serious Play)
Explore the issues relating work and leisure. Develop a personal leisure ethic based on examination of leisure interests, options, and community resources. Develop a plan for exploring leisure options in your home community.

Volunteering and Community Involvement
Discover the benefits and various options involved in community
service. Develop a plan for exploring local service options at home.

Work Portfolio Options
Consider various forms of paid work including starting a small
business, consulting, shared work, or part-time and seasonal work.
Develop an information gathering and job search strategy. Students also leave with a portfolio of their talents.

Semester #2 — Planning

Physical, Mental, and Social Wellness
Plan for maintaining physical, mental, and social health across
the different stages of a second career. Learn about avoiding the
most common senior illness, depression, and how to sustain and
nurture one's spiritual and social needs.

Financial and Survival Strategies
Plan for the future and rethink the definition of "success," as well
as budget secrets and investment ideas. Examine materialism and
consumption in later life and methods for scaling down both.

Finding Your Story and Developing a Second Career Plan
Review your life story, developing journaling techniques. Develop
a personal portfolio, autobiography, or scrapbook. Learn career
goal-setting and information-gathering techniques.

Sharing and Application ... Year 2

Semester #3 — Culminating Project Work

Teaching Assistance
Serve as a teaching assistant or peer support to first year program.

Project Seminar
Develop project (thesis) for culminating experience. Develop com-
petency or completion checklist which includes work on attitude,
physical health, and a program of learning or using talents.

Semester #4—Presentation of Culminating Project

Project Completion
Review project and make final preparations.

Culminating Project Presentation
Finish project and present to staff and student body to receive degree.

Million Dollar Idea #2: Starting a Leisure Club

S THERE A way to pursue leisure wellness in the company of others? Could the leisure search be conducted in a support group similar to a job club? What about the possibility of joining a club where you can meet people with similar leisure-wellness interests or find people who want to gather to start informal leisure activities like a journal writing group, book club, antique-repair collective, etc.

All of this could be yours. You *can* band together with others to form a club that promotes serious play.

People would be admitted to the club after completing an orientation class on leisure wellness. One could use this book, local speakers, or other resources to structure an eight-week course that would help people acknowledge the importance of balancing work and play, and assist in making plans for leisure wellness. During this class, students would assess their leisure interests, preferences, and values. They would set goals for leisure wellness and conduct a leisure search in teams as described in Chapter 6— The Leisure Search.

At the end of the class (which would require both a commitment of time and money, in the form of course fees) the student would earn a membership card entitling them to one free month of membership. Thereafter, membership would be sustained by both dues and participation. You will have to determine the appropriate vehicles for participation for your community and members. The following list will help you get started in deciding upon your club's activities.

Monthly (or Weekly) Leisure-Search Support Meetings

People who are still looking for local opportunities meet to discuss their leisure search experiences. This would be modeled after various job-search support groups. Participants review what they completed the previous week, brainstorm new places or people to visit, and make plans to search with others when possible. They hear speakers from various local groups or other members at large in the leisure club.

Some groups with a special focus may want to meet weekly. A leisure search support group might be formed for at-risk youth, retired people, people recovering from drug and alcohol addictions, widows, new community members, etc.

Ad Hoc Special Interest Leisure Associations

These are ad hoc or informal (perhaps temporary) associations formed of people with similar interests. They fill the gap when people can't find a club to join which suits their interest. For example, suppose someone wants to join a low-cholesterol gourmet club, a journal-writing and book-reading club, weekend walking club, or a singles go-to-the-movies club. When no such groups exist, leisure club members create their own ad hoc group or club by advertising in the newsletter or on electronic bulletin boards. They try to form a group committed to meeting at least three times to try out the idea.

Semi-Annual Club Meetings

All active, dues-paying members are invited to semi-annual events, usually potlucks with displays of club members' current leisure-time involvements. There might be a guest speakers, comedians, magicians, or other performers, slide shows, or panel discussions. The evening ends with various opportunities to play and socialize—games, a dance, or coffee and music.

Newsletters

A newsletter could be very important to sustaining member involvement and recruiting new people. This newsletter would provide an alternative to the "personal" ads found in today's papers. As a result, people in your community are no longer limited to meeting people with similar interests through these ads and other dating-type services. In your newsletter, people would advertise their leisure interests and preferences in hope of finding others with similar orientations. You don't have to be a single person to advertise; you can have many different reasons for wanting to find people with similar leisure interests.

Perhaps you can talk your local newspaper into giving you some free space to help you get started. It could be a very valuable community service. If the newspaper likes the effect, they may invite your club to run this as a regular column. You can also explore the possibility of electronic bulletin boards and local access cable channels.

The newsletter could also feature interviews of club members, advice columns, and information about upcoming events. It would be a great place to inform your readers about other local leisure opportunities in schools, clubs, organizations, etc.

While the club would be open to anyone, it would usually attract people at midlife through retirement. Therefore, you must decide if you truly want it to be an intergenerational program and plan accordingly. Good luck in your endeavors and write to me (in care of the publisher) when you get a club started.

Electronic Bulletin Board/Database

A similar "connecting point" can be established by creating an electronic bulletin board where people can share similar leisure interests via computer. Alongside this, a database is compiled of all members' interests. As with a match-making service, one can look for a person with similar interests.

Meeting people who share your interests is never easier and safer than when you meet them through a concept I call "The Electronic Leisure Connection," a way of finding friends using a computer plugged into a modem and connected to an on-line network.

Electronic networks are powerful, but they are also daunting. This limits the audience greatly. It probably is the reason a number of people decide to disconnect, soon after subscribing. Currently, to use even the most user-friendly network one must climb a lengthy learning curve before reaching the plateau where the fruits of cyberspace can be sampled and enjoyed. As a simple example, there are about five different ways to get help on one of America's easiest-to-use networks. And the Internet ... well I have better things to do with my leisure time.

Let's face it, once a "newbie" successfully logs on for the first time, he or she faces the blinking riddle, "Now what?" E-mail is fine, if you have someone to write to, and who writes back. Chat or live talk (typing) sessions are exciting if you are talking to someone who shares a common interest.

My leisure-connection concept would put the newcomer in touch with a potential friend in the blink of an e-mail.

Giving People a Leisure Address

In the past, finding someone with, for instance, a similar interest in wood-carving, first required several initial sessions just to master the language of networking. I have, however, devised an ideal model for how bulletin boards might better serve the needs of leisure-searchers. What follows is a best-case scenario for how this might work.

In my model everyone completes a short "leisure profile," which includes their leisure address. This address identifies a person's interests and talents. It is based on a self-administered leisure interest questionnaire, and it becomes the gateway to others.

Upon completing the questionnaire (Kimeldorf's Leisure Options Inventory) a person chooses a brief alpha-numeric code or address. For instance, the following letters could be used: E-Entertainment, O-Outdoors, G-Games, V-Volunteering, to name a few. Within a given area like volunteering one finds many subsets of leisure possibilities—maybe V-9 for volunteering in schools or V-45 for volunteering in food banks. People can use these leisure addresses or codes to find a kindred soul.

The wise network provider could end up with one of the largest leisure matching services in America. This could be the right time for such a service, as the aging population goes in search of meaning and fulfillment outside of their traditional work roles. It would also serve special-needs groups: divorcees, widows and widowers, mid-life searchers, and people working through other problems that require human dialogue. The following scenario illustrates how all of this might play out.

A Typical Scenario

Maurice works all day in a large state agency. As a middle manager he has come to master word-processing and databases on the office computer, but he's never had much interest in on-line activity.

Maurice recently attended a preretirement seminar and learned that people who fail to develop interests and contacts outside of their workplace tend to find the transition to retirement very difficult—and to lead shorter lives. Because of the recent budget cutbacks, he feels that he has probably reached a career plateau. Therefore, he is now involved in a midlife reevaluation. Mo, as we'll call him, has concluded it is time for a change. In the past he has lived to work; now he wants to work to live. Mo feels something is missing in his life. He knows that he has many unused talents and interests. It is time to explore!

His wife bought him this book, hoping it would help him get through this rocky late-life passage. He read with interest about the five ways in which career choices are intertwined with leisure life choices. As a workaholic, he responded to the passage about people abusing their free time. By the end of the book, Mo felt he had a firm grasp of "leisure wellness." At the seminar, he also received a copy of a disk from a progressive network company which promised to connect him to a leisure network—without the pain of learning cyber-techno-babble.

The software on the disk was a simplified shell or interface for the network, dedicated to the subject of leisure and the task of connecting with other members. The slogan that greeted new users read, "Putting the human face before the Interface." The disk software was designed to introduce newcomers to the opportunities of joining an electronic community. The software took Mo right to the menu for the Electronic Leisure Connection.

Mo completed the leisure interest questionnaire on the computer screen and found that his main interests were located in the leisure clusters labeled "1) Games and Friendly Competitions." Within this cluster, Mo could choose from thirty representative leisure activities. He wanted to explore the Japanese board game of go, a strategic game something like chess. He started with the category for these kinds of games which was eighth on the list. This gave him his first code or leisure address: G-8. Mo went on to identify two other areas he was interested in, to insure that he had balance and options.

Mo completed a short registration form which logged him on to the network. In his user profile he entered his three leisure codes. The computer responded by asking if he wanted to download a list of up to ten people who shared his interests. He hit the "enter" key and was taken to the e-mail introduction letter. Mo then sent off letters to the people who came the closest to his specific leisure interest.

Next, the software took Mo to the Electronic Leisure Want-Ads Bulletin Board. Here were leisure ads, or postings, grouped by the previous cluster scheme. At first, he just randomly surfed across the boards. One person was looking for a book about journal writing, another for the name of a good park to fly kites in, and another wanted to find someone who knew how to repair fly-fishing reels. In his next session, Mo returned to the games bulletin board and posted a message. Then he moved into one of the forums where people chat in real time.

Eventually Mo met someone who played both chess and go. After sending some e-mail, Mo finally connected with a go-game master. The next month Mo bought his daughter a modem for her computer. He winked at her and they both laughed; they knew who really wanted the electronic gadget.

People in the helping professions also found uses for the leisure network. Psychologist Latoya Fromm suggested that her rehab clients plug into the Electronic Leisure Connection. She felt that many of the clients had difficulty forming new lifestyles, friendships, and interests once they gave up a lifestyle based on drugs.

Another psychologist recommended the network based on her research into the beneficial effects of membership in electronic communities for people suffering from depression.

Each week brought more stories about people finding new uses for the network. Ellen, who was recently divorced and not yet ready to start a serious relationship, was a bit lonely, and wanted to meet another person who shared her interest in philosophy and poetry. The Electronic Leisure Café was an easy place to plug into on a Friday night ... friendly and safe. It was like meeting some-one in a bookstore café. She liked it so much, Ellen bought her recently widowed mother-in-law a subscription to the network.

Using Leisure Wellness in Drug Treatment

By Curtis Rosler

ATTENDED MARTIN KIMELDORF's first leisure wellness workshop with the notion that I might discover fun things to do as well as the motivation to actually do them. I quickly sensed that the term "leisure wellness" was not just a catchy title for a workshop, but an important concept that I needed to examine in my life. I continue to ponder the concept to this very day. What I heard and felt during that workshop produced ideas and plans of a really different sort. I have since applied the concept to my work as a counselor in a chemical dependency treatment center. Not too long after the workshop experience, I decided to float the idea of "leisure wellness" with the clients I serve in the fifty and older group at our chemical dependency treatment center. The group responded to the message immediately. That early success led to a new workshop series in our twenty-one day treatment program.

I developed a series of three two-hour workshops to help residents at our facility examine the role that leisure plays in their life. In this way, we hope that each person will leave with a set of leisure goals which will strengthen the overall recovery plan. I believe that leisure education and counseling are crucial ingredients in the recovery process. The person who successfully abstains from alcohol or drugs is suddenly faced with a great challenge: filling their new drug-free hours with healthy activities, attitudes, and (new) friends. In this appendix, I'll show you how I orient a new resident to the concept of leisure wellness. I'll illustrate this in a mock-orientation with fictionalized names and end with a brief summary of the exercises and sequence I use in my workshop.

Mock Orientation

Anderson Chemical Dependency Treatment Center is nestled in
a wooded area, adjacent to a small Pacific Northwest city. Today,
I am greeting Larry and giving him the initial orientation to the
center, with a particular emphasis on the leisure workshops I offer.
Larry admitted himself to the center after experiencing family
problems which led to a separation from his wife. During intake
he admitted to consuming four to five sixteen-ounce cans of malt
liquor per day, and more on the weekends. While he has tried to
quit many times, Larry has only been abstinent for one week in
the last year. He is college educated and works as a supervisor in
a large health and social service state agency. Larry explains that
he is frustrated and angry. Many times during our conversation
he blames others for his current predicament.

I review with Larry the facts of addiction. I tell him, "Addiction is a process that effects the physical, emotional, social, and
spiritual health of our patients ... and their families." He grows
quiet. His gaze shifts as he stares out the window and nods his
head as we recount the problems. I then point out that our program offers medical treatment for the physical damage, education about the nature of addiction, and individual and group
therapy about life issues and leisure wellness. We discuss the fact
that support from family, friends, and peers will be important as
he embarks on an extensive behavioral change. "It will mean that
you spend the rest of your life in recovery. Are you ready for
that?" I ask. Larry looks up, and takes aim at me with his unblink-
ing eyes, "I feel like I've hit bottom. I need help. I want my life
back!"

I continue, "While you are in treatment, I want to invite you
to attend my three workshops about leisure wellness. This should
give you new tools with which you can reshape your life." Larry
thinks for a minute, "How will this leisure workshop help me?"
I know that asking questions is a good sign. I elaborate, "Larry,
during the first part of rehab you're going to have to face off
against some very large questions. You might be asking yourself

things like, 'How will I ever get through this? Will I get back on my feet? Will my wife take me back?' And, if you stick with it and develop a plan for abstinence, then you face another difficult question as you heal: 'How can I have fun now that I've given up drinking?' I think this workshop will help you find answers to these questions. You're going to learn that just as you abused drugs, you also abused your free time." Larry slowly nods, "You're right. I filled every free moment with a can of malt liquor." I then assure him that he will find a way to create a new and healthier leisure lifestyle. I point out, "You are going to be suddenly faced with many new free hours. Some people are haunted by these hours. I want to show you how to fill your leisure time with options which can ignite your soul and stir the passions."

Larry makes eye contact; I know I've made the connection. I go on to describe some of the things he can look forward to doing in the workshops: "In this first workshop you'll be asked to go back to your childhood and examine leisure pastimes you enjoyed—without drugs. We'll connect the remembrance of your healthy past with a vision of your new, wholesome future. Many people find this recollection process painful at first, but later describe it as therapeutic or healing. Next, you'll take an inventory or assessment of your current state of leisure wellness, your leisure preferences, and values. You'll be taking stock of your leisure values and interests. You'll pick three new leisure activities to investigate, and finish up by considering how to balance work with play and home obligations." Larry now begins asking about the details, "Why do I need to pick three?" I answer, "By coming up with more options, you won't end up trading an addiction to alcohol for an addiction to a singular leisure activity, like computers or jogging."

It is important to end this orientation with a stern note of caution. I explain that the failure to design a set of lifestyle alternatives just increases the risk of relapse after inpatient treatment. I conclude by pointing out, "Larry, any lifestyle change will only be effective it you feel passionately about where you want to go and what you want to become. Let me help you rekindle your sense of curiosity as you set a new course, a new purpose."

It was after the second workshop that Larry took me aside. There in the long quiet corridor, he discussed his recent realization that as a result of using alcohol he had lost contact with the hobbies he once enjoyed. He concluded, "Once I get started doing something in my free time that I really enjoy, I'm sure I'll find the key to recovery." He left the treatment facility with enthusiastic plans to join a computer club, play chess again, and browse regularly through local bookstores. At our final family conference, his wife acknowledged this new beginning with many agreeable nods of her head. She then voiced some concerns which Larry dealt with honestly. She touched a tissue to her eyes just before she embraced Larry. Then they began discussing reconciliation.

On Larry's last day, he thanked me for the extra time I had given him. His wife, who is a very artistic person, left a special card with gold foil and a calligraphic message reading: "All I need lies within." Larry later sent me a separate thank-you note in which he wrote, "It's hard to explain how much comfort your conversations have brought me . . ." I consider these items to be my leisure studies diploma.

Syllabus

This is a brief outline of the exercises which I use in my group sessions. Many times, the written exercises are completed individually and then later discussed at large. The conversations which follow the exercise often take off in unpredictable, but fruitful, directions. The two hours go by so quickly, we leave always wanting to talk more. The following scenario is based on an early version of Kimeldorf's book; as a result, the actual titles in this book may be slightly different. However, this should give you a feeling for the overall sequence of my workshops.

Workshop #1:
Defining Leisure Wellness; Redefining Leisure
Introduction
Group warm-up game.

Defining Leisure (see page 7)
Discussion:

- Share definitions of leisure
- How does our free time reflect our values and interests?

Leisure Quiz: How Do People Spend Their Leisure Time? (see page 8)
Discussion:

- Why does saying, "I'm bored" lead to both relapse and problems with leisure wellness?

The Leisure Wellness Survey (see page 11)
Discussion:

- How can you look at your results without judging yourself?
- How does chemical dependency affect each of the five areas?
- Define Leisure Wellness or the notion of balance in life.

Treasure Chest Recollections and Future Projections (see page 85)
Discussion:

- Point out that recollections such as these can involve some pain.
- Does your current definition of leisure fit your recollections?
- Begin sharing hopes and dreams.

Good News/Bad News Visualization (see page 88)
Discussion:

- Get wild; really brainstorm!
- Explore various questions in depth ("who would you take," and creative replies).

Workshop #2:
Examining Styles and Preferences

Review previous session.
Group warm-up.

Leisure Style and Preference Inventory (see page 99)
Discussion:

- What are your strengths and weaknesses?
- What opportunities do you see for change in your life?
- How has chemical dependency interrupted your leisure life?
- Why are the categories of people, places, and time important?

Kimeldorf's Leisure Options Inventory (see page 106)
Discussion:

- What old leisure interests did you mark?
- What new ones would you like to learn or take a risk to explore?
- Which activities are affected by chemical dependency?
- Fill in three new leisure options in your Personal Recovery Plan.

Workshop #3:
Integrating Leisure Wellness into Recovery

Review previous session.
   Talk about the importance of balancing work and family and leisure.

Balanced Leisure (see page 126)
Discussion:

- Add any new ideas into your Personal Recovery Plan.

Conclusions

As I write today, it has been two years since I began teaching leisure wellness at our center. People who have successfully completed the treatment program repeatedly tell me that the leisure wellness class was one of the most important experiences during treatment. They specifically mention the exercises which explored the pleasant experiences in their past. Larry once observed, "It was a time when I could play and become totally absorbed in an activity, without drinking or using."

As a drug and alcohol counselor, I find it very important to link yesterday's recollection of fun with the future possibilities. One of my tasks is to help people rediscover the words "play" and "fun" in a drug-free life. One way I facilitate this discovery is to adapt an exercise Kimeldorf uses in his workshop which emphasizes the importance of taking one's play seriously. I ask my clients to join with me in a short exercise called the Mirror Game, in which people pair up and try to mirror every move made by their partner. What begins as a serious attempt at concentration soon breaks down under a storm of tumultuous laughter. As the laughter subsides, I ask our group if they are ready to once again have fun without drinking and using. A thoughtful silence fills the room. I point out that we need to talk more about the "F" word ("fun"). The group then embarks on a series of discussions guided by the questions: "Is work the absence of play? Can your play be your work? How can you achieve a balance between paid work, leisure, and chores?"

Note: Curt Rosler did an outstanding job of interpreting my materials for his clients. He covers a great deal in a short space of time. If Curtis could expand his workshop I would then suggest that he add sections on the actual leisure search as found in chapter 6.

—Martin Kimeldorf